MUSIC AT ITS BEST:
THE BERLIN PHILHARMONIC
FROM KARAJAN TO RATTLE

Books on Demand

To Hagen Michael I and II

Title of the German version:
Berliner Philharmoniker. Von Karajan bis Rattle
Updated in 2009
Translation: Allan Mitchell and Annemarie Kleinert
Copyright © Annemarie Kleinert
Published in Norderstedt, Germany
www.BoD.de
ISBN 978-3-83706-361-5

Contents

3   Claudio Abbado as Artistic Director: 1990 - 2002   45

4   The Orchestra on Tour   60

Preface

The Berlin Philharmonic, one of the most prominent orchestras in the world, has a long history. Founded in 1882 it quickly became known as the leading institution for classical music. Mostly from 1955 onwards, after Herbert von Karajan became its artistic director and with modern technology advancing at a rapid pace, it even gained an unsurpassed recognition among non-experts.

This short history mainly covers that last period. It has taken advantage of a large number of photographs made by a former orchestra member, Gustav Zimmermann, who always had his camera next to his violin during rehearsals or concerts. His archive made me realize the rich background of the topic.

In addition, I was able to gather a few pictures by other artists, that is: by Cordula Groth, wife of the former orchestra member Konradin Groth (pp. 35, 43, 53, 100, and 131); by Jürgen Dibke, who followed the orchestra on tours (p. 79); and by Karsten Schirmer (bookcover) whose father Ludwig was one of the few photographers accepted by Karajan. The medal on p. 17 belongs to Rudolf Weinsheimer, a former cellist of the orchestra. My thanks to them all.

I am also grateful to some people whose advice or proofreading helped to finish the book: to a number of former or present orchestra members, namely Gustav Zimmermann, who collaborated with me over months; the solo-drummer Rainer Seegers; the violinists Hanns-Joachim Westphal, Madeleine Carruzzo, and Walter Scholefield; the cellist Alexander Wedow; and some musicians who did not wish to be mentioned. Among the non-orchestra-members I want to thank Helge Grünewald, head of the administrative department of the orchestra; Beate Burch-hard, former manager of the Easter Festival in Salzburg; Rosemary Ripperger and Jürgen Dibke, for years keen admirers of the orchestra; Annemarie Vogt and Isolde

Hamprecht, musicologists; Barbara Gobrecht, founding member of the *Hochrhein-Gesellschaft der Freunde der Berliner Philharmonie*; Jutta March of the archive of the Berlin Philharmonic; and also Hagen and Michael Kleinert, my husband and son, who were of great help during technical difficulties with the computer version of the manuscript.

The book first came out in German, then in Japanese.[1] The American translator of the first draft, my friend and former colleague Allan Mitchell, whom I met during my teaching time at the University of California at San Diego, suggested rendering the name of 'Berliner Philharmoniker' as 'Berlin Philharmonic'. Like big cities (Rome, Munich), great orchestra names deserve translation.

Annemarie Kleinert, Berlin, May 2009

1

The Berlin Philharmonic, its Building and its Organization

An appropriate name has been useful for many an artist. But it must be clear and resonant.

Not until 2002, when the orchestra's organizational structure was transformed after creating a foundation, did the *Berlin Philharmonic* acquire a steadfast title. Throughout many decades the musicians played under different names: either as the *Berliner Philharmoniker* (whenever they performed as a private organization, for example when they recorded music), or as the *Berliner Philharmonisches Orchester* (at concerts as the official representatives of the city-state of Berlin). To make the confusion total, all of this occured in a structure called the *Berliner Philharmonie*. Hence the familiar anecdote: A visitor in Berlin asks someone on the street: 'How do I reach the famous Philharmonic?' The answer: 'Practice! Practice! Practice!'

1.1 Home: The Philharmonic Building

A concert hall is as important for an orchestra as studios and galleries for painters to exhibit their art. A new residence was necessary after the Second World War because the former one, the old Philharmonic building in the Bernburger Straße, next to Potsdamer Platz, had been destroyed in bombing raids towards the end of the war. The orchestra at first appeared in various municipal concert halls, but that was only an unsatisfactory solution. In 1960 a new edifice was finally approved, which was initially to have been constructed near the Kurfürstendamm, on property now occupied in part by the Freie Volksbühne. Eventually it was planned in the center of Berlin, again near the Potsdamer Platz. Unexpectedly, during construction, the Berlin Wall was erected in August 1961, so that the building at its completion in 1963 stood on the eastern edge of West Berlin. Not until the opening of the Wall twenty-eight years later did the position again occupy the center of the city's activity - maybe one reason why building and orchestra were called in 2008 by a newspaper, when a minor fire broke out, 'The Heart of Berlin'.

Still fascinating today is the architecture of Hans Scharoun's cement structure, covered on the outside by pale gold protruding aluminum panels and distinguished, among other features, because of the irregular play of steps and terraces inside and out. Pathbreaking at the time was the positioning of the podium inside, not at the end of the hall but rather closer to its center. Thus out of a maximum audience of 2 446 people, 270 can sit behind the orchestra and nearly 300 on each side. Scharoun wanted to emphasize the communality of musicians and listeners. The audience should, said Scharoun, 'be distributed in nine levels as on terraces of a vineyard' with the conductor's podium approximately central in the 'valley'. With its complex balconies, tiny round windows, and white metal surfaces, the labyrinthic landscape of the foyer recalls the decks of a luxury liner (Scharoun spent his youth close to a port).

Adjoined to the concert hall in 1987, following the original ideas of Scharoun (who died in 1972) and completed by his partner Edgar Wisniewski, was a similarly conceived building for chamber music, which is connected by a gallery with the main hall.[2] The funding came in part from the *Society of Friends of the Berlin Philharmonic*, a registered organization since 1949 that had already collected considerable sums for the great concert hall. With its 1 195 seats, the newer hall is notably large for presentations of chamber music. In contrast to the first hall, the second has cellar areas with room for a parking garage. There is also a storage room for musical instruments. On the grand floor of the main building several larger instruments are likewise stored along with travel cases in the substage. For years Berliners called the complex of large and small buildings the 'Circus Karajani', because Karajan was longtime the chief conductor of the orchestra and because of the tent-like roofs of the halls. Others speak of the 'City crowns on Potsdamer Platz', in reference to the pointed gabels on both rooftops.

At its opening many criticized this architecture as all too unwieldly, and they worried about the acoustics, which in fact did not meet expectations. But after the installation of reflecting panels and elevation of the podium, the acoustics were so outstanding that the Berlin Philharmonic now enjoys a worldwide reputation as possessing one of the best concert halls. The broad steps of the podium in the great concert hall are adjustable, and the entire area can be lowered to create an orchestra pit.

From January 1991 to April 1992, and again for two weeks in May 2008, the large building was closed for necessary repairs, especially of the concert hall's ceiling. During this time the orchestra played in other concert houses, among them the one on the 'Gendarmenmarkt',[3] an imposing sumptuous structure conceived by Friedrich Schinkel in 1818, whose inner space is impressive. The musicians also had performed there in May 1989, with the direction of James Levine, under entirely different circumstances. At that time

Figure 1.1   The Philharmonic building in Berlin was a pioneering architectural achievement at its inauguration in 1963: as in some ancient amphitheaters, the orchestra is practically surrounded by part of the audience. The idea has been imitated by more recent constructions throughout the world.

the location belonged to the communist controlled part of the city, which was difficult to reach for residents of the western section. During a short bus ride over the existing border, along the Berlin Wall with its guard towers and barbed wire, everyone had an oppressed feeling. Yet, the concert hall was sold out.

1.2   Hierarchies in the Orchestra

The orchestra employs 129 musicians, but some posts remain unoccupied, so that the actual number of orchestra members somewhat varies. As a rule there are between 40 and 50 violins (in 2008 there were 42), about 14 violas, 13 cellos, 11 bass strings, 38 brass instruments, as well as 4 percussion instruments and 2 kettledrums. When the orchestra was founded in 1882 it had only 54 members.

Although the musicians are equal, there are professionally established hierarchies. Naturally the concert masters have a special role (in the Berlin Philharmonic they belong to the first violins - in some other orchestras also a second violonist may have that title). Through them a necessary close contact is provided between orchestra and conductor. For example, before rehearsals, they agree on the repetition of certain passages in order to perfect rhythm, phrasing, and tonal balance. They also play violin solos from such pieces as *Heldenleben* by Richard Strauss or Rimsky-Korsakov's *Scheherazade*. For the string instruments they regulate the bowing to assure uniformity. Last but not least, they give the signal to the entire orchestra for the tuning of the instruments. The Berliner Philharmonic has three 'first concert masters' and one 'concert master'.

The solo musicians of the second violins are called 'tone leaders' (*Stimmführer*) or 'lead players' (*Vorspieler*), of which there are three. Other groups also have their leaders: the violas, cellos, bass strings, flutes, oboes, clarinettes, bassoons,

horns, trumpets, and trombones. When instruments are
played by a few musicians, or even a single one like the tuba
or the harp, there are no special solo instrumentalists. Hence
all musicians must master their own solo passages. Seldom-
used instruments such as the saxophone are as a rule handled
by musicians of other instruments (for the saxophone, for
instance, it is a clarinettist). For the piano or the organ, the
orchestra has no regular staff but only irregularly engaged
artists. However, since 2002, a pianist-in-residence is invited
each year to collaborate with the large orchestra and the
chamber music groups.

1.3   Seating Order of the Philharmonic

The disposition of the Berlin Philharmonic on stage is
ordinarily arranged according to the so-called 'modified
American' scheme that has been for decades preferred by
many symphony orchestras. In contrast to the older German
pattern, the second violins sit between the first violins and the
cellos, while the violas have a place at the right-hand front
side. Some conductors (for example Nikolaus Harnoncourt)
occasionally employ the German seating order where the cellos
have a central position.[4] At filming sessions with Karajan,

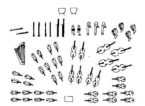 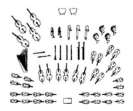

Figure 1.2   Orchestra placement: on the left, the 'adopted American'
seating arrangement; on the right, the 'traditional German'. The
distribution may be slightly changed whenever more instruments are
added (for example, extra harps in Wagner's *Walküre*).

who usually had himself filmed from the left because he found that more flattering, it was necessary for the cellos and violas to change place - otherwise leaving the modified American seating intact. Sergiu Celibidache wanted the cellos to his right because he considered it important to maintain close contact between violins and violas.

As is well known the concert masters and soloists always sit up front. However, it may be unknown to many concertgoers that among the larger groups of instruments there is no fixed place reserved for the 'tutti'-musicians (tutti = Italian for 'all'). For a given program, to be sure, each keeps the seat assumed at the first rehearsal. Only a few 'tutti'-players - usually older ones - have by consent the right to a certain seat. New members, at least one time in the first year of their probation, sit next to each of the players in their group in order that their artistic talent and harmony may better be judged.

1.4   Tuning of Instruments

The tuning of instruments is an interesting ritual that every concertgoer knows, though the details of it are usually ignored. It is necessary before - and sometimes again during - every rehearsal and every concert. When all the musicians are seated, the concert master calls by a gesture or by rising for quiet, and he requests the lead oboe player to sound the note 'a'.[5] In case of a piano concert, the 'a-tone' is struck on the piano. If the score does not include either oboe or piano, the note is played by a flutist or clarinettist. Some musicians have their own electronic device for controlling the 'a'. Occasionally, when different instrument groups - for example, woodwinds and horns - are not in harmony, the concert master will call for an electronic 'a' to be played. In that event, the note emanates from an area near the stage entrance. There sits at least one of the four technical assistants, who also controls the lighting, temperature, and humidity of the concert hall and who oversees activity on stage by video-cameras.

1.5   A Democratic Institution

Since its foundation in 1882, members of the Berlin Philharmonic have organized themselves democratically - an extraordinarily long period of self-government that is to be explained by the initial situation. The orchestra arose through a protest of 54 musicians against their conductor, Benjamin Bilse, who had since 1842 directed the original orchestra in Silesia (after 1867 in Berlin) in a very authoritarian manner. The protestors created their own orchestra with statutes that would never allow such conditions again.[6]

The basis is clearly the so-called orchestra assembly, which can last several hours and in which all musicians are bound to participate. The chair is occupied by two elected orchestra members plus a committee of five. Since 1952, when the orchestra became affiliated with the municipal government of Berlin, the staff council also has a saying when it comes to some decisions.

The duties of the two main officers are various. In close contact with the chief conductor and the administration, they must arrange nearly forty programs per season, assign all instrument groups for roughly a hundred performances a year, supervise rehearsals, gather opinions concerning tours, and represent the Philharmonic in public. On tour, they generally assume responsibility for travel arrangements. And it is they who convoke assemblies of the orchestra.

The committee of five is important for the atmosphere of the orchestra. Among other things, it collects opinions of the members about special questions, for example guest conductors or invited soloists. The staff council mainly

Figure 1.3 The orchestra is one of the oldest musical institutions organized in a democratic manner. Here during the election of a new chief conductor.

represents the interests of the musicians in contractual questions.

An important theme of the orchestra assemblies is the initiation of new musicians, which often creates heated debates. For instance, at the outset of the 1960s, Karajan wanted absolutely to engage a horn soloist whom the orchestra, after a year of trial, chose to reject. At the time, the conductor made use of his veto, but after some back-and forth he relented and accepted the decision.[7]

The democratic structure is also evident in the choice of a new chief conductor. Long debates over the candidates occur and secret deals are made. All of this very stressful and exciting activity is overseen by a barrister. After Karajan submitted his resignation in April 1989 - about three months before his death - the selection of a new chief conductor was held at the Siemens estate[8] on October 1989. This procedure behind closed doors had all the pomp of a papal election.[9]

1.6   Female Members of the Orchestra

Since September 1982 women musicians also belong to the Berlin Philharmonic. For a whole century it had been a 'Republic of Males', as the orchestra was sometimes called. Madeleine Carruzzo was only 26 years old when she read about a vacancy in the magazine *Das Orchester*, and soon thereafter she auditioned. Altogether there were nearly a hundred candidates, since many are interested especially in applying as violinists. A preliminary selection netted 13 musicians who were invited to a test performance. Some

Figure 1.4 A century after foundation, in 1982, a woman was for the first time employed in the orchestra: the violonist Madeleine Carruzzo (left Riccardo Muti).

of them came from the *Orchestra Academy of the Berlin Philharmonic* that has existed since 1972 (see page 38).

The young female musician, who hailed from francophone Switzerland, explains how she had to gather courage for such a test performance because of the Berlin Philharmonic's unsurpassed worldwide reputation. Karajan had made it more internationally recognized than ever before, and Carruzzo admired many of the orchestra's members who were famous soloists. In the announcement stood only 'We are seeking a violonist' and not as is usual 'a first (or second) violinist'. Since auditions went in alphabetical order, she was among the first to play (a Mozart violin concerto and a Bach sonata). She learned that afternoon that she and another candidate would be welcomed to the group of the first violins.

This offer was especially important for her because she could encounter the most prominent of guest conductors and soloists, and that in the largest city of Germany. Moreover, she had the opportunity to travel with the orchestra on tour throughout the world. Her contract was likewise financially attractive, and it would offer tenure after a successful year of probation. By now, Madeleine Carruzzo has been at home in Berlin for more than 27 years.

Unlike most other orchestras, all musicians of the Philharmonic plus the chief conductor and the head of the administration decide together on the engagement of members, not just the lead players or a small group of them. For that reason also an audition for tenure, after years of probation, is always held in front of the entire orchestra. Carruzzo learned that, besides musical qualities, much depended on the total impression made by a candidate, who must fit in with the 'family' of the Philharmonic, as Karajan put it, including appearance as well as personal and professional attributes. Initially the 'First Lady' noticed that her colleagues sized her up more carefully than male beginners.

Other appointments of female musicians followed, among them that of Sabine Meyer (who had appeared as a substitute with the Philharmonic several months before Madeleine and who thus had in a sense already broken the ice). In September 1983, Meyer's appointment for a probationary year occasioned a dispute between the orchestra and Herbert von Karajan with far-reaching consequences (see p. 36). But this is forgotten now. About 12 percent of positions are held by female musicians, some of whom on probation. Even in groups of instruments like the horns, in which women seldom play, female talents are no longer unusual.

1.7   Daily Contacts

Of course, the most time-consuming duties of musicians are the almost daily rehearsals. From 10 a.m. to 12:30 and, if no performance is on the program, also from 4:15 p.m. until 6:45 there are usually rehearsals in the large concert hall of the Philharmonic (until 1963 these were held in the common room of a Protestant church in Berlin-Dahlem). Also on weekends rehearsals occur whenever the schedule of performances requires it.

During rehearsals a casual atmosphere exists on stage, since members are playing in front of empty seats. They wear daily clothing like sweatshirts and jeans, handbags hang from chairs, and on the floor lie music scores or small instrument cases. Yet, despite this apparent relaxation, everyone concentrates. Usually the rehearsal is suspended for a pause of twenty minutes. Some conductors use part of this time at the pulpit to answer questions. Others hasten immediately to their dressing room to freshen up from the strain. Or they lounge in the cafeteria near the stage door. Musicians either remain at their place, making penciled notations in their score, practicing fingering without a sound, or discussing with colleagues. Themes are the next towns to visit on tour or the quality of an instrument they want to acquire and which they have brought with them.

These days almost all instruments are property of the individual musicians, apart from a few large ones such as bass strings and drums. Originally that was otherwise: many instruments belonged to the orchestra, not only for financial reasons. It was assumed that a unified tone would be better attained by purchasing instruments from the same craftsman, especially brass instruments. But this custom has lapsed, partly because more musicians in the course of time could afford expensive instruments (Stradivaris, Guarneris, etc.), and partly because different nuances of tone are unavoidable (especially among the strings) even when they have been obtained from the same manufacturer.

Daily life goes on partly backstage. There rooms are available for the different music groups as well as for the chief conductor, guest conductors, and invited soloists. The largest rooms are occupied by the string and brass players. On the tables, which are covered with velvet to protect the instruments, are other things besides instruments: reading material, skat or chess games, and sometimes food and drink. Each member of the Philharmonic has his locker in which he keeps his tuxedo, black shoes and suits for matinees, and his instrument if it is not too large. In the early years after the war, so-called tuxedo-money was available for the purchase of the required clothing. Also important for the musicians are common rooms on the top floor and quarters of the administration on the second floor of the Philharmonic building. Parts of the administration are housed in the 'Kollhoff'-building nearby on the Potsdamer Platz.[10]

Parties are sometimes arranged in the large music rooms to celebrate awards to individual musicians, birthdays, or New Year's, and also when someone has died or when a musician retires. Responsible for the arrangement of such occasions are the honorary officers of the *Association of the Berlin*

Figure 1.5   The orchester occasionally performs with non-experts of classical music, as here with the chansonnier Udo Jürgens (left) and the master of subtle comedy Vicco von Bülow.

Philharmonic (Gemeinschaft der Berliner Philharmoniker),[11] who also speak at funerals and Christmas parties. At Christmas retired members of the Philharmonic and their spouses are invited along with distinguished guests from the world of art and politics.

The former president of the *Bundesrepublik*, Richard von Weizsäcker, was often present at such celebrations. Since his childhood he had been connected with the Berlin Philharmonic, for which he has served as an executive member of the sponsoring committee in 2002. He has given speeches in the Philharmonic hall, among them a very moving address at the observance of German unity on 3 October 1990, after Kurt Sanderling conducted works of Bach, Haydn, and Brahms. Likewise, Vicco von Bülow, that master of subtle humor and longtime friend of the orchestra, is occasionally to be seen with the musicians. „Loriot" - as he is called - has participated in several programs, for example at the Chancellor's ball on 6 October 1979, when he performed a comedy sketch involving a piano mover bothered by a nervous insect, who accidentally stumbles to the conductor's podium and who inadvertently waves his arms just at the right moment to direct the orchestra. In 1993 he published an audiotape in which he impressively commented on Wagner's *Ring of the Nibelungen* as recorded by the Berlin Philharmonic under Herbert von Karajan from the years 1967 to 1970.

1.8 Honors

Many awards have been given to people affiliated with the orchestra. The *Association of the Berlin Philharmonic* gives three: the honorary membership (among others to Senator Joachim Tiburtius and agent Erich Berry); the golden honor ring, a symbol of fidelity to the orchestra (for instance to Wilhelm Furtwängler and Karl Böhm); and also, since the 1970s, the golden Hans von Bülow medal, named after Hans Guido Freiherr von Bülow, the first great conductor of the musicians (see p. 74). Among the recipients of these medals are guest conductors Seiji Ozawa and Bernard Haitink,

Figure 1.6 Awards given by the orchestra to distinguished personalities: the golden ring of honor and the Hans von Bülow medal with the logo of the Philharmonic.

soloists Rudolf Serkin, Claudio Arrau, and Yehudi Menuhin, the singer Dietrich Fischer-Dieskau, the longstanding chief administrator Wolfgang Stresemann, and the musicologist Hans Heinz Stuckenschmidt. Honorary medals and rings are also awarded to all members of the orchestra who have served in the Philharmonic for at least thirty years, which is often close to the time of their resignation. On such occasions the usually reserved Karajan always found a generous word of thanks, sometimes on the verge of tears.

Among the prizes awarded to the entire orchestra or earned by soloists and conductors are honorary citizenships, artistic mentions, honorary degrees from universities, and medals from federal and state governments (e.g., the *Bundesverdienstkreuz*). Furthermore, members and associations of the Berlin Philharmonic have been received by academies and awarded prizes by private firms or clubs, for example the Würth Prize, the Ernst von Siemens Prize, the Grand Prix du Disque, the Edison Prize, the Grammy Award, the Prize of German musical record critics, the Herbert von Karajan Prize, the Urania Medal, and prizes commemorating various composers. Musicians like Abbado and Rattle possess so many awards, rings, medals, and other honors that they can scarcely recall where or when they received them. Among the distinguished recordings by Rattle with the orchestra was Mahler's *Tenth Symphony*, an unfinished work reconstructed by the musicologist Deryck Cooke and completed by Berthold Goldschmidt, Colin Matthews and David Matthews. This record was awarded the prize of German music record critics and a Grammy in September 2001.

1.9   Recordings

As mentioned, not too long ago musicians of the orchestra produced recordings of disques or videos privately, that is, each of them was paid separately for devoting extra time to working with the orchestra.[12] That is no longer the case. Whether musicians perform in concert or for recordings, they do so as members of the Berlin Philharmonic Foundation.

Within the orchestra, representatives of the media have an important role because they provide contacts to recording firms, radio and television companies, as well as film, video, and DVD productions. Since the presence of these representatives is not insignificant, their additional activity is remunerated.

Not all recordings occur at the Philharmonic hall. Studios are sometimes rented, and films are shot at Berlin's elegant halls like the Siemens estate or the Charlottenburg castle. Earlier, many records were produced in the Jesus Christ Church on Thielplatz, known for its excellent accoustics, located in the verdant southwestern sector of Berlin-Dahlem (on occasion this church is still used today). While Karajan was working with the orchestra there, all windows had to be closed to avoid noise from wind and airplanes.

At recording sessions musicians are able to learn the eccentricities of invited soloists. For instance, the violinist Shlomo Mintz always had his instrument-maker with him to assure perfect tuning. Luciano Pavarotti often made comic grimaces with his tongue and facial muscles before singing. And the Austrian singer and composer Udo Jürgens felt honored, his own popularity nonwithstanding, to be asked for autographs in June 1979 when he recorded his eight-minute composition *Word* with the Berlin Philharmonic.

Like Jürgens, the orchestra won at this time a golden record, that is, the *Deutsche Grammophon* awarded one of them to each of the 119 musicians for their recording of Beethoven's Fifth Symphony. Later the firm awarded only smaller gratuities.

Before the fall of the Berlin Wall, a chorus from East Berlin sometimes appeared for recording sessions in West Berlin. Possibly one or another singer may have thought

Figure 1.7 Luciano Pavarotti and James Levine at a recording session with the orchestra. On the right Pavarotti while practicing before the recording.

about defecting. But probably no one wanted to endanger another's special permission that had been granted for the appearance. Besides, according to regulations, only married chorus members were allowed to enter the West.

1.10   The Administration

The Berlin Philharmonic has a constitution requiring self-government. But since 1935 a chief administrator (*Intendant*) collaborates in the organization of performances (except shortly after the war - 1945 to 1951; and again between October 2002 and July 2006, when F.X. Ohnesorg prematurely resigned). The fact that an *Intendant* exists is partly due to the bad economic interwar times endured by the orchestra. It goes back to the period of National Socialism.[13] Shortly after the Nazi seizure of 1933, the orchestra was placed under the Ministry of Propaganda and its members became for the time being functionaries of the Reich. A politically reliable person was chosen to be the chief administrator. The Jewish concert agency of Hermann and Luise Wolff, which had made many business arrangements, no longer existed.

The *Intendanz* is also a convenience. It manages guest appearances, visiting conductors, and soloists, as well as many technical and administrative matters.

Many musicians have said that one of the most important such administrators was Wolfgang Stresemann, son of the legendary Chancellor and later Foreign Minister Gustav Stresemann (1878-1929). Repeatedly he understood how to reconcile in a diplomatic manner Karajan's special wishes with the democratic format of the orchestra. He also supplemented the program initiated by his predecessor Gerhart von Westerman with contemporary music under the title *Music of the Twentieth Century*, so that modern classics became more emphasized. After leading the orchestra's administration for 19 years, he left the Philharmonic in 1979 at the age of 74. But six years later the orchestra turned to him again after the quarrels over Sabine Meyer. So Stresemann remained again for two more years.

Several chief administrator have followed.[14] The one who came in 2006 is a woman, Pamela Rosenberg. Her experience in Amsterdam, Hamburg, Frankfurt, Stuttgart, and San Francisco, plus her sense for teamwork and her vision of the future, are her prerogatives for success. She does not want the orchestra to be an elitarian club but a group of musicians playing for people of all kinds of social and ethnic backgrounds. Her contacts to the main sponsors of the orchestra (since June 2002 mainly the Deutsche Bank) are excellent.

1.11   Chief Conductors since the Orchestra's Founding

Naturally the leading personalities are the chief conductors. In 125 years since the orchestra's founding there have been only a few, because some passed decades with the orchestra, especially Arthur Nikisch (27 years: 1895-1922), Wilhelm

Furtwängler (31 years: 1922-45 and 1947-54), and Herbert von Karajan (almost 35 years: 1955-89). Some conductors remained only a couple of years, such as Hans von Bülow from 1887 to 1893 (he died in 1894). Only two conductors have received an unlimited contract: Furtwängler at the age of 65, two years before his death, after he had already conducted the musicians for nearly three decades; and Herbert von Karajan, who from the beginning of his contract was installed without limitation - albeit somewhat vaguely 'more or less for life'.[15]

Furtwängler is still well remembered by a few retired members of the Philharmonic. After he had been chief conductor from 1922 to 1945, the political situation after the war had required his temporary resignation.[16] From 1947 until his death in 1954 he conducted again in Berlin, since 1952 as 'conductor for life'.

During the brief postwar interim the orchestra was provisionally taken over by Leo Borchard, who had often conducted the Philharmonic before the war (1934-36). He seized the initiative amid a general chaos in May 1945 by collecting the scattered musicians. Unfortunately in August 1945 he was shot by a military guard at the English-American demarcation line in Berlin while seated in the automobile of a friend driving him home from a party - a victim of the nightly curfew.

Borchard was followed by the 33-year-old Romanian Sergiu Celibidache. Furtwängler much appreciated this nearly unknown man with the intense eyes, who had until then been a university student in Paris and Berlin. The musicians were also enthusiastic about the professional maturity of Furtwängler's protégé, who always directed from memory without a score. But vigorous disputes arose over everyday matters in which he proved undiplomatic. For example, the aging of the orchestra became a topic when the very idiosyncratic conductor complained that the average age was higher than in other orchestras - a result of the fact that

Figure 1.8 Sergiu Celibidache, postwar conductor of the Berlin Philharmonic, at a rehearsal with the musicians: an encounter after 38 years (March 1992).

musicians had not been inducted during the war. By now the age structure of the orchestra is comparable to others.

In the past two decades about eighty new positions have been filled that had become vacant for reasons of age or illness. Occasionally, for instance on concert tours, retired musicians have been temporarily engaged, among them the former leader of a violin section, Hanns-Joachim Westphal, who at the age of 71 traveled with the orchestra to New York during his fiftieth year as a member of the Philharmonic. That was in September 2001, shortly after the terrorist attack on the World Trade Center, when the active members of the orchestra had to worry whether they should risk a flight over the Atlantic.

After Furtwängler's return to the pulpit of the Berlin Philharmonic in 1952 which ended with his death in the midst of preparations for a first tour of America in 1954, Herbert von Karajan, at the time the foremost German conductor, was asked whether he would come to Berlin. In stark contrast to the more passionate Furtwängler, Karajan was considered a somewhat 'cooler' representative of classical music, meeting the demands of modern times. It soon became apparent that he had the talent and the finesse to lead the orchestra to greater heights.

2

The Era Herbert von Karajan

Chief conductors, it is said, are the center of an orchestra. Some concertgoers and older members of the Philharmonic still remember the Karajan years as the most brilliant period. He was not only a remarkable musical talent with a large repertoire, but he also fascinated by his charisma and had the gift of effectively staging performances. His long and continuous collaboration cemented the worldwide reputation of the Berlin Philharmonic.

2.1   A Man with Many Qualities

When Karajan was asked by the musicians in December 1954, during preparations for a planned trip to the United States, to take over the direction of the orchestra, this was the beginning of a nearly 35-year collaboration with him as chief conductor. Soon his name and that of the Berlin Philharmonic appeared frequently in the media.

He was also mentioned in the press for non-musical reasons, because of his abilities as a superb manager, his hobbies as pilot of private jets and helicopters, or as an excellent skier, as well as his success with society ladies (he was often seen with film stars and his three marriages were notorious).[2] Always a favorite object for press photographers, he appeared at events of High Society.

2.2   The Maestro is Everywhere at Home

The quality of Karajan's conducting and his media presence meant that his concerts were regularly sold out. Hundreds of Karajan's fans stood waiting for hours in ticket lines. However, he disappointed the orchestra at first, soon after signing a preliminary contract in 1955, by not hesitating to pursue, besides his obligations in Berlin, time-consuming engagements in other countries, especially in Austria, but also in Italy, England, and Switzerland. In Austria he occupied responsible posts as artistic director of three important institutions: the Vienna State Opera, the Vienna *Singverein*, and the Salzburg Festival. Often he appeared with the Vienna Philharmonic and made elaborate tours. Moreover, he regularly conducted the opera of La Scala in Milan, recorded with the London Philharmonia Orchestra, and appeared on stage with the Swiss Festival Orchestra in Lucerne.

Austria was actually the center of Karajan's life. In Vienna alone he was under contract for seven months a year, and two more months were devoted to the Salzburg Festival. As a consequence there was relatively little time left for Berlin. Symptomatic of this situation: he had no residence in Berlin but lived in a hotel suite reserved for him, for a long period in the Savoy, later in the Kempinski on the Kurfürstendamm. At the same time he owned homes in Salzburg, Saint Moritz, and Saint-Tropez.

Karajan's secretary André von Mattoni has said that Berlin was for the maestro at the outset, in contrast to Vienna 'simply a vacation'. In fact, the conductor came each year to Berlin at first for only six scheduled concerts and for New Year's, also of course to accompany the orchestra on tour. True, he rehearsed intensively in the few weeks of his presence and also did recordings, but altogether the musicians had only sporadically the possibility to discuss important matters with

him. Berlin concertgoers thus regretted the meager presence
of their Philharmonic's chief conductor.

2.3 Practice, Practice, Practice

With the 1964/1965 season the situation changed when
Karajan left the Vienna State Opera. Thereafter he was
able to devote himself more frequently to the orchestra in
Berlin, and members of the Philharmonic clearly noticed the
difference. The following fifteen years marked the highlight of
Karajan's work with the orchestra.

He achieved this because he ran a tighter ship than others.
His nimbus was so great that the musicians already inside the
rehearsal room perceived his arrival before he entered the hall.
Without mercy he demanded only the best from everyone,

Figure 2.1 After Karajan's appointment as chief conductor in 1955,
the already active travel program of the orchestra also lead to far away
countries. Here the arrival in Japan in 1966 (left in profile, one of the
elected chairs of the orchestra, the cellist Rudolf Weinsheimer).

including himself. That was the case even in later years when
he was suffering from health problems.

Respect of the orchestra's musicians was based on
Karajan's admirable self-discipline and reliability, his
exactness in following plans, his empathy, his passion, and
his grasp of every instrument. Listeners throughout the
world spoke of the enchantment produced by the orchestra's
especially beautiful tone. In sum, Karajan stood for classical
music of the highest quality, and his musical philosophy
remained for years the foundation of the orchestra.

2.4   Relentless Rhythms

Above all, Karajan had a perfect ear for the most subtle
rhythmic nuances. He was so proud of this sensitivity that
he often claimed: 'I can circle the Philharmonic building and
be back exactly a given time.' Some musicians thought that
impossible and criticized him as a precision pedant. Others
believed him and assumed he possessed an inner metronome.
Again and again he went through certain passages, for
example Ravel's *Boléro*, with the percussionists Fred Müller
and Gernot Schulz, in order to attain the utmost precision
in this respect. In any case, tempo and intonation as the
essence of musical expression and form were for him principal
concerns.

2.5   Karajan's Gestures as Conductor

Karajan passed through various phases in his manner of
conducting. His initial youthful élan was reported in the
press, as when for instance three days after his thirtieth
birthday, on 8 April 1938, at his first appearance with the
Philharmonic. He dominated the orchestra with expressive
light movements of the wrist, and every concertgoer sensed the
elemental passion of his musical leadership and his boundless

energy.[3] In an interview he remarked that he was aroused
by the easily expressed discipline, the adaptability, and the
intelligence of the musicians, as well as their sense of humor,
which led him to imagine that a perfect symbiosis would be
possible.

Thereafter a phase in his career ensued in which his
outstanding personality and classical aesthetics made every
performance into a show. He conducted with such vigorous
gestures and an often so transfixed facial expression that his
admirers were extraordinarily touched. Critics wrote that
works conducted by him would breathe.

In a later phase he came to a more sublimated manner. It
sufficed to raise his eyebrow or to nod his head in order to coax
the almost ethereal beauty from a score. Despite back pains
and other ailments he was able to achieve greatness for the
musical world, remaining present with every fiber of his body
and enobling musical works with his superior understanding
of them. The result was described as a tone of 'velvet and
silk'.

2.6 Without a Score

There was in fact no member of the orchestra who did
not admire Karajan's professionalism in the prime of his
career. His phenomenal memory for all things musical was
legendary. At rehearsals he sometimes quoted Hans von
Bülow's statement: 'A musician should not have his head in
the score but the score in his head.' He himself knew from
memory every detail of the music even when the program
consisted of works very different in style. He always conducted
at performances without a score - which is extremely difficult
especially with compositions like Stravinsky's *Rites of Spring*
- and most passages with eyes closed. This habit drew the
anger of Adolf Hitler at a presentation of *Die Meistersinger
von Nürnberg* at the Berlin State Opera that he conducted in

June 1939. One leading singer was momentarily indisposed and had to skip an entire passage, forcing the orchestra to adjust with him, thereby creating confusion. The Führer let it be known thereupon that he would never again enter an opera house if Karajan directed without a score.

During the Salzburg Easter Festival the maestro was in addition in charge of directing the stage (only in 1975 and 1987 did he allow productions by other directors, namely Franco Zeffirelli and Michael Hampe). He rehearsed so much that the position of every extra in the chorus and every spotlight on stage was realized exactly as he had planned. Nothing escaped his notice.

2.7   The Private Person

As to Karajan's character, even today the members of the Philharmonic are of different opinions. Some praise his interest in their private affairs. He often asked about the hobbies of his musicians or in case of medical complications put them in touch with outstanding physicians, for example when professional accidents or illnesses occurred (such as orthopedic or auditory problems). Others had no access to him and found him egocentric, unable to put up with his moodiness and his often dictatorial ways, especially in the last years of their collaboration. He was 'in love with himself', as they said. They also wondered about small details, for instance that in his dotage he almost never put on reading glasses although that would have been useful in some situations. Instead, Karajan followed the Italian composer Spontini, who gave Wagner the advice never to wear eye glasses while conducting, no matter how nearsighted he may be.

Some musicians criticized that Karajan hardly ever tolerated differing opinions about the interpretation of difficult passages. If anyone found it necessary to express a contrary viewpoint, the maestro could be very sharp. 'It is difficult, if not impossible, to conduct a conversation with Karajan on music,' said the former administrator Wolfgang Stresemann.[4] However, the maestro had the ability at this time to motivate the orchestra like no other conductor, to guide the musicians before performances whenever they were nervous, and to concern himself about the psyche of each individual.

2.8   A Reserved Man

Karajan's reputation of keeping his distance from most people is well known. His occasional attempts to overcome that trait were unsuccessful, as when he attempted to imitate Karl Böhm's usual heartfelt bow to the public after a concert. Böhm succeeded in stirring enthusiasm by turning to the audience with open arms as if he wanted to embrace them. When Karajan tried to imitate this specific gesture, it fell flat. For this rather unapproachable man such action was perceived to be all too artificial. He nevertheless enjoyed rousing applause.

Perhaps this reserve - some say this shyness - even contributed to his fame. His appearance gained the distinction of a genius totally concentrated on his craft. He sometimes needed complete inaccessibility, for example when filming. During breaks he would put himself into a sort of space capsule where he would hide out in the middle of the stage. It was round, compact, and had no windows. Some musicians speculated that he practiced yoga inside. 'You recover your inner balance through yoga, try it,' he was often heard to say.

That he withdrew in later years during rehearsal intermissions is understandable, because the loud confusion during pauses usually is hard to endure. Chairs and music stands are moved, difficult passages rehearsed, conversations conducted. Such noises can be unpleasant for a musical ear.

2.9   Enthusiasm for Technology

Karajan displayed a special talent in the use of modern technology like records, film, television, and later videocassettes and CDs. Through these media the *Karajan Miracle* (as the journalist Edwin van der Nüll already called him in October 1938) became known worldwide by a large public. The importance of these technologies was recognized by him immediately after their invention. In 1962, for example, he and the orchestra became pioneers through the introduction of stereo recordings of all nine Beethoven symphonies presented on different tapes and offered in a beautiful box.

Also his assistants, agents, and advisors (André von Mattoni, Uli Märkle, Ronald Wilford, and Michel Glotz) were particularly gifted in the popularization of the so-called 'serious music'. The Berlin Philharmonic averaged 24 recordings a year with Karajan, which naturally contributed to his strong attachment to the musicians. These recordings appeared mostly with the Deutsche Grammophon, but also with EMI-Electrola,[5] and less often with DECCA. In 1982, Karajan founded his own film firm 'Télémondial' (earlier he had worked with 'Unitel'). Even in comparison with younger conductors who grew up with modern audio technology. His catalogue of records, film, and television productions is still unsurpassed (about 800 recordings and 90 video performances).

Karajan's enthusiasm for technology may have derived from the fact that he spent the first three semesters of university at the *Technische Hochschule* in Vienna before changing to music as his major. At recording sessions the 'boss' was equiped. He followed the registration with earphones, communicated with technicians by telephone, and meanwhile naturally led the ensemble with his baton. He also carried a stopwatch to make exact corrections of certain passages. When CDs came onto the market, he displayed the new apparatus during a press conference at the Salzburg Easter Festival in 1981 and declared that - unlike conventional records - this new machine did not alter the tone of music when turning it up side down. Karajan and the Philharmonic inaugurated the era of digital recordings with Richard Strauss' *Alpensinfonie*. 'Everything before that is gas lamps,' said Karajan at the time. The Berlin Philharmonic recorded two of the first operas on CD, *Die Zauberflöte* and *Parsifal*. The development of technology was obviously a pleasure for Karajan.

Whenever films were made during concerts and loud coughing could be heard in the hall, scenes needed to be repeated at great cost. The maestro personally spent entire nights at the editing table. The result was that he could well evaluate such work. He consequently praised the accomplishment of good technicians in front of musicians.

Through their many recordings Karajan and the orchestra won prizes that of course caught the attention of more amateurs and sponsors of the Philharmonic. The artistic director was able to draw in numerous leading business personalities to finance expensive productions, above all in Japan. To make such arrangements, he frequently met patrons during concert tours. The maestro thus communicated the flair of a man in a hurry and yet immensely efficient.

Naturally, he consciously reacted to certain experiences of the orchestra. That was quite clear in 1979 when the musicians performed Mahler's *Ninth Symphony* with Leonard Bernstein as guest conductor (see pp. 85 ff). Shortly thereafter Karajan prepared a recording of the same piece. But in the final movement, after a fortissimo passage following a pianissimo, he had the orchestra play notably louder than Bernstein, as if he wanted to distinguish his own interpretation from that of the American.[6] He offered no explanation to the musicians.

2.10   Relation with Fellow Conductors

Karajan considered Bernstein to be one of his greatest competitors. He closely followed every step of his American colleague, and vice versa. Each wanted to outdo the other on an international scale. In the initial years both avoided meeting for different reasons, yet secretly they admired one another.

Before Karajan assumed a leading position at the Berlin Philharmonic, the competition with Furtwängler was also of great importance to him. Naturally he regarded him with utmost respect and was doubtless disappointed that Furtwängler evidenced little concern. But he never managed to be treated with comradeship. When he succeeded Furtwängler, after the latter's death, Karajan wanted to distinguish himself. Some members of the Philharmonic reported his saying 'enough of this old hat' whenever worn habits stood in the way of his instructions. For instance, when raising his baton to begin a piece of music, Furtwängler would leave his arm dangling in air for an instant. The players in the bass strings, whose instruments were slowest to sound, would begin the motion of their bow before the others. This habit was not easily altered, a bother to Karajan (as well as some guest conductors like Rafael Kubelik). Repeatedly Karajan attempted to make clear that he alone was to signal the downbeat and not any group of instruments. And actually his gesture at such an important moment was more decisive than Furtwängler's. To compensate 'this old hat', some members of the Philharmonic at first overreacted by beginning a fraction of a second too late.

Figure 2.2 The signature of Herbert von Karajan shows his strong personality.

2.11 Karajan and the Paparazzi

Karajan was highly critical of photographers with whom he had bad experiences. Some waited for him in the dark, blinded him with their flashbulbs, and then published unflattering pictures. He therefore made it mandatory that every photo had to be approved by him before publication. If someone printed a photo without approval, he could fall into disfavor. Some musicians and singers fared likewise if they were insensitive enough to cause his anger. When he was older, trust turned sometimes into hate, and according to Wolfgang Stresemann there was even a black list.[7] One of Karajan's methods to treat differences with musicians was to accord them fewer solo passages at important concerts or recordings. Some photographers considered him to be hypersensitive.

2.12   Disputes in the Final Years

During the 1980s there were increasing disputes in Berlin between Karajan and the musicians. Above all this was the result of his refusal to accept unquestioned some democratic decisions. For his elitist character unions were a thorn in the side, because they might enable imcompetent persons to determine policy and cause funds or titles to be falsely allocated.

One example suffices to make the point. A general tendency in the 1970s among Berlin bureaucrats was to extend privileges to many persons (functionaries automatically received a raise in pay every second year and it was even suggested to pay students a salary). It was thus proposed to bestow the title of *professor* to each member of the Philharmonic. Karajan struck up an alliance with the Berlin senator Adolf Arndt while standing before the musicians and saying: 'If everyone receives something, it is the same as if no one receives something. Gentlemen, the title of member of the Berliner Philharmonic is better than that of a professor.' The majority of the orchestra agreed. Anyway, some of its members already had professorial rank in a university music faculty.

The case of Sabine Meyer created a major quarrel for Karajan. The twenty-two year old clarinettist had become known to the Philharmonic in 1981 as a temporary replacement for an indisposed soloist. Shortly thereafter, a position to succeed Ulf Rodenhäuser became available, for which she applied. However, the orchestra decided against accepting her for a probationary year. Despite that, on 16 January 1983, with the help of administrator Peter Girth, Karajan arranged such a contract for her, beginning in September 1983. This action contradicted the democratic statute of the orchestra. The details of the ensuing public conflict have become insignificant by now since Sabine Meyer was only engaged by the Philharmonic for barely eight months (from September 1983 until 12 May 1984). She renounced her contract, as she said, 'in order to avoid further conflicts with incalculable tensions'. But what remained was a shattered relationship of trust between the orchestra and its - now almost octogenerian - artistic director. He was deeply wounded by the entire affair. Members of the Philharmonic took afront at his cancellations of scheduled concerts and his insistance on already fixed decisions. The estrangement grew.

Because this trouble kicked up waves in the press and injured both parties, mutual encounters became less frequent. A genuine reconciliation that might have altered the maestro's attitude never occurred. Symbolic of this relationship was the appearance in October 1987 of a Mozart record for the benefit of young AIDS victims *without* a conductor. Increasingly impatient, Karajan turned more and more to the Vienna Philharmonic, and he surrounded himself with young musicians and great singers, notably the Bulgarian soprano Anna Tomova-Sintov and the American Jessye Norman. They became - together with his wife Eliette, his children, and the Karajan Foundation - the important companions of his final years.

2.13   The Maestro and Young Talents

Throughout his life it was a major concern of Karajan to discover new talents. Whenever he succeeded in doing so, he was enchanted, warmhearted, and openminded. He frequently emphasized, however, that they must be extraordinarily trained, technically and musically, not simply talented.

Seiji Ozawa was one of the protégés who profited from Karajan's vast experiences. Gundula Janowitz and Leontyne Price were also advanced to many a famous stage thanks to his active support and authority. Likewise exemplary was his initiative in founding the *Orchestra Academy of the*

Berlin Philharmonic, which was created in 1972 with grants for young instrumentalists who had finished their formal musical studies or who had similar qualifications. The main sponsor was the Dresdner Bank. The so-called 'Orchester-Akademie' is still today located in Berlin, where about thirty scholarship students a year receive as a rule 24 months of private instruction from concert masters, group leaders, and soloists of the Philharmonic. Occasionally they are allowed to play at rehearsals and concerts and are eligible whenever vacancies at the Philharmonic are announced. Nearly 25 percent of the approximately 80 new appointments since 1990 have been students from the Academy. In case they are not accepted, they still have an advantage over others in finding a prestigious position (more than 50 percent have gained a leading post in large orchestras). The goal of the Academy is to transmit its traditional ideas of musicianship. So far about 600 prominent musicians have been produced by the Academy.

In like manner, Karajan's support for the gifted violinist Anne-Sophie Mutter has made history. His first encounter with her was in 1976 at the Lucerne Festival. She was only 13 years old and was appearing with another orchestra. An invitation to audition with the Berlin Philharmonic followed. Alas for her, that ended with the depressing decision that her young talent was not yet mature enough and that she should return a year later. At the second audition in the spring of 1977 something like a spiritual bond developed between her and Karajan. Anne-Sophie was allowed to appear on stage with the Philharmonic during the Salzburg Whitsun Concerts. Karajan also saw to it that a sponsor provided her with a Stradivarius violin.

After February 1978 Anne-Sophie Mutter was often a guest with the orchestra in Berlin. Even sceptical musicians were astonished how the teenager endured such pressure with a light touch. Their enthusiasm persists to this day.

Figure 2.3 Karajan supported gifted young talents. Here in 1980 with Anne-Sophie Mutter (r.) and with his wife Eliette at the Easter Festival in Salzburg.

'You could ask what you wanted of her, Mozart, Vivaldi, Beethoven, Mendelssohn, Tchaikovsky,' said the violinist and orchestra member Gustav Zimmermann, 'she took up each piece easily, managed all the nuances masterfully, and made fluent transitions from one part of a work to another'. The opinion was unanimous that it was a pleasure to hear her perform and to feel the youthful spirit and warmth that she exuded.

Karajan soon made her his favorite, appreciating above all her technique with cadenzas, that is the difficult solo passages that demand everything from a violinist, for example the Joseph Joachim cadenzas. The maestro arranged an exclusive contract for her in Berlin by which she appeared there only with the Philharmonic. Her calendar was soon fixed years ahead of time. It was sometimes hard to tell whether she accompanied the orchestra on tour or vice versa (e.g., to Tokyo in 1981).

When in 1984 differences arose between Karajan and the Philharmonic, and the orchestra did not appear at the Salzburg and Lucerne Festivals, the violinist sided with Karajan and played in Lucerne without remuneration in order, as she said, 'to help reduce the overhead that resulted from the Berlin Philharmonic's absence'. At the inauguration of the Philharmonic chamber music hall in Berlin, on 28 October 1987, she was heard once more as soloist in Vivaldi's *Four Seasons*. But it was the last time she was seen with the Berlin Philharmonic in that century. When she played there again in February 2002, it was at first without an orchestra, only in a trio with the cellist Lynn Harrell and the pianist Lambert Orkis, an unusual event in a sold-out large concert hall for only chamber music. In 2003 she returned to the orchestra under the conductor (and composer) André Previn, her second husband, in subsequent years under the artistic direction of Simon Rattle.

The last child prodigy that Karajan sponsored, in 1988, was the Russian pianist Jewgenij Kissin (born in 1971). Karajan was already acquainted with the young man through live recordings dating from 1984. He met him personally at the Salzburg Festival in 1988 and spontaneously invited the 17-year-old for a New Year's concert in Berlin and at Easter 1989 in Salzburg. For Kissin it was the beginning of a meteoric career. The New Year's concert, carried on television, would be for Karajan his final appearance with the orchestra in the building of the Berlin Philharmonic.

2.14   The Herbert von Karajan Foundation

The maestro envisaged a number of new projects, of which several were never realized. There was thus a rumor that he had found wealthy patrons who would provide the

Philharmonic with valuable instruments. Nothing came of it, but from his private fortune emerged in 1968 Berlin's *Herbert von Karajan Foundation.*

As the Foundation's constitution states, it should serve above all 'the promotion of young artists, scientific research, and international resonance in the field of music'. Various projects were - or still are - under this Foundation, for one, from 1969 to 1985, the bi-annual conductor's competition in Berlin. Among others, Dimitri Kitaenko, subsequently director of the Moscow Philharmonic, was a winner of this contest, as were the Latvian Mariss Jansons (see p. 100), and the Russian Valery Gergiev, later artistic director of the Mariinkij Theatre in Saint Petersburg. In the last four years of his life the maestro continued this aspect of the Foundation somewhat differently. He advised qualified musicians personally in conducting - for instance during guest tours to Leningrad, New York, and Tokyo - and supported some of them with fellowships. After his death in 1989, such fellowships were still granted in combination with university music programs. Further competitions for conductors with prize money from the Foundation were held in Weimar in 1999 and Lübeck in 2004.

A second project of the Foundation ran from September 1970 to the beginning of the 1980s, also in bi-annual cycles - each time gathering ten youth orchestras in Berlin. At their conclusion, a youth orchestra composed of the best members of the competing ensembles was assembled, with which the maestro performed a farewell concert on television.

The third project, which existed for decades, was scientific research in music and medecine. Since Karajan's father had been chief physician at a Salzburg clinic, the musical son was naturally interested in the effect of playing and hearing music on body and soul. Especially encouraged was the heretofore little investigated discipline of musical therapy, pursued since 1969 with cooperation of doctors and psychologists, at first from the university of Salzburg. Other funded projects included 'The relationship between intelligence and musicality', 'Music and sleep', and 'The psychological effect of pop-music on youth'.

Academic symposia were organized for years at the end of the Salzburg Easter Festival by Karajan's physician Carl Walther Simon. These forums had for example the motto 'Time in music' (1983). Karajan took an active part in such presentations.

Much later, at a first world congress in 1996, the Institute of Music Therapy was founded at the *Hochschule für Musik und Theater* in Hamburg. It bears Karajan's name.[8]

2.15   Resignation in April 1989

As Karajan's health noticeably declined in 1988, while he suffered from the effects of an infection as well as earlier operations and a stroke, a gathering crisis developed between him and the orchestra and above all between him and Berlin politicians.

The Socialist-Green coalition had the discourtasy to criticize openly the often honored recipient of awards, medals, and prizes - among which an honorary citizenship of Berlin in 1973. They said that he had grown too old in office and could no longer entirely fulfil his duties, for example, that he was not regularly present at auditions of musicians for important posts, that he accompanied the orchestra less often on concert tours, and that he was frequently absent from Berlin for months at a time. Karajan therefore demanded his obligations and rights be clearly defined, since they were insufficiently explained in his contract. No answer was forthcoming.

The humiliated maestro reacted violently. On 24 April 1989, barely a month after his last performance in Salzburg with the musicians (Verdi's *Requiem* on 27 March 1989), he submitted in writing his resignation as artistic director of the orchestra. He handed this letter to Senator Anke Martiny, who had hurried in anticipation to Salzburg to calm the conductor down. Karajan had in fact the right - ever since reaching the age of 65 and not 81 - unilaterally to submit his wish to retire at any moment. But it was the painful insult of the heartless Senate that brought the end.

Figure 2.4 A bust of Karajan by Kurt Arentz in the Austrian embassy in Berlin (on the left the author of this book). Another bust of Karajan (by Hans Bayer) stands in the foyer of the Berlin Philharmonic, a third one at the cemetery in Salzburg-Anif where he is buried.

2.16   July 1989: Death of the Maestro

Most members of the Philharmonic were crestfallen at this unexpected step and felt orphaned after so many years of collaboration. Karajan remained mostly at his home in Austria from April to the middle of June 1989, presumably

with sadness and pain from the dissolution of such a long
relationship. One day before his resignation he had conducted
a Sunday matinee of the Vienna Philharmonic in the famous
Musikvereinssaal of that city. It was his last appearance in
Europe. Scarcely three months later, on 16 July 1989, he died
at his home in Salzburg-Anif (see p. 120). The Italian Claudio
Abbado, born in Milan and then general music director of the
city of Vienna, would soon become Karajan's successor in
Berlin.

'His performances almost always have the aura of a creative act'.
(Christian Försch)

3

Claudio Abbado as Artistic Director: 1990 - 2002

It was for a much shorter time than Karajan (12 years rather than 35) that Claudio Abbado worked with the Berlin Philharmonic as its chief conductor. But he inspired many in the public so much that for them no further embellishment of musical pleasure seemed possible.

His appointment as artistic director after Karajan's death was nearly simultaneous with the fall of the Berlin Wall, exactly a month and a day before the stirring events of 9 November 1989, namely on a sunny Sunday afternoon of 8 October 1989, as the East German regime was celebrating its fortieth and last anniversary. The general atmosphere of liberation would soon bode well for a cultural renaissance in the formerly isolated city. Hence Berlin was not just the focal point of an epochal political transformation but a musical one as well.

3.1 Time for Changes

The Berlin Senate supported projects that emerged from this historical situation. After decades, musical facilities in West Berlin were now also available for previously excluded residents of the Communist East. The majority of the western public was likewise infected by this euphoria and looked with anticipation to its classic trophy orchestra.

Certainly, innovation did not occur quite as rapidly as many had hoped after the upheavals - partly due to the currently unsatisfactory circumstance in the years before Karajan's departure. True, the orchestra spontaneously organized a free matinee concert in the Philharmonic building for guests from East Berlin on Sunday, 12 November 1989, but for this performance Claudio Abbado was not yet available (it took place with the conductor and pianist Daniel Barenboim, who happened to be recording works of Mozart with the orchestra).

Contractual negociations of Abbado with the Senate lasted until September 1990. The musicians gained positive impulses from guest conductors, but a firm hand of one's own, a unified policy, and a coherent inspiring personality were lacking to lift the orchestra and dissipate everyday routine. In addition, several orchestral positions were vacant and the Philharmonic building was damaged - a part of the ceiling had collapsed - which meant that concerts had to be held in other halls until 1992.

3.2   Abbado's Earlier Appearances

Abbado and the Berlin Philharmonic had already been acquainted for more than twenty years. He had been invited to Berlin seventeen times - beginning on 20 December 1966, six years after his debut as conductor in Milan - and he had altogether given thirty-six concerts there.

Many of the members of the Philharmonic first learned details of his background during his election, for example that he had studied with Hans Svarovsky and had been for a year Leonard Bernstein's assistant with the New York Philharmonic; also that he was discovered in 1964 by Karajan at a concert of the American radio channel RIAS in Berlin with its Radio Symphony Orchestra and was thereupon invited in August 1965 to the Salzburg Festival with the Vienna Philharmonic. Very significant for his popularity, moreover, was his appearance at the Munich Olympic Games in 1972 with the orchestra of Milan's Opera La Scala, whose musical director he had become in 1968. Furthermore in his curriculum were important positions in Vienna, Chicago, and London.

Figure 3.1 Claudio Abbado becomes Karajan's successor. The statue of Furtwängler in the south foyer of the Philharmonic seems to approve. In the background the former senator Anke Martiny and the violinist Hellmut Stern.

3.3 A New Repertoire

Whereas Karajan's repertoire included above all the 18th to the early 20th century, with only occasional excursions to modern works (for instance Berg, Schönberg, Penderecki,

Ligeti, Orff, and von Einem), Abbado increasingly began to turn to contemporary composers like Nono, Henze, Stockhausen, and Rihm.

He and the chief administrator proceeded carefully with the composition of programs. They brought new music together with classics and often created a relationship through a common literary or historical theme. The critics were enthusiastic, the conservative public less so. At concerts one could observe during modern works how some persons sneaked out of the hall whenever unfamiliar tones were sounded; or, whenever a modern piece was played at the beginning, how audience members only arrived after the intermission. But Abbado's cleverness gradually succeeded in making the musical avantgarde more popular, as when for example admission to general rehearsals was allowed or jazz musicians like Wynton Marsalis appeared with the Philharmonic.

Another change was that many musical scores from the outer reaches of the classical repertoire were played, discarded original versions of frontier classics, or forgotten compositions from earlier epochs of musical history. Abbado is well acquainted with the historical background of music. If possible he inserts original instruments into Monteverdi or other composers of early baroque, for instance, when substituting the usual harpsicords with lutes, or he chooses a small ensemble as was earlier customary in royal courts and salons. Established habits of listening were thus placed into question. He was helped in this policy by several soloists such as the Italian piano virtuoso Maurizio Pollini and the Austrian pianist Alfred Brendel.

3.4   His Interpretation of Music

Naturally, in addition, the program offered often played classics, which are a challenge with any change from one chief conductor to another. That was true of Abbado, who

struggeled to introduce something of his own besides the
interpretations of the 'beautiful Karajan tone'. An example
was Karajan's very elegant rendition of Beethoven's Second
Symphony, which he had interpreted with very quick tempo
to emphasize its unified broad resonance. In contrast, Abbado
was more reserved, set softer accents, and allowed pauses to
achieve an 'inner breath'. By reconsidering many details, the
music assumed different contours.

There were also classical works that Abbado made more
lively, since he was a passionate man who preferred some
pieces in more rapid tempo. 'Typically Italian', was the
public reaction.[2] Generally his manner of conducting tended
less to pathos and his interpretations were 'more transparent',
according to the cellist Alexander Wedow. With Mozart he
wanted some passages to be played 'senza vibrato', and the
mentioned smaller orchestra ensemble meant that the sound
was not too ample. Under Karajan there had usually been
too many rather than too few musicians.

Abbado's preference for smaller groups probably results
from his tendency to see only chamber musicians when facing
a large orchestra. As he explained in an interview for
this book: 'Everyone in the Berlin Philharmonic is of great
talent, each a great chamber musician. It may be that it
has something to do with the democratic tradition of the
orchestra. As in a chamber orchestra, the players listen more
carefully to one another. And this attitude also affects guest
soloists. They feel like part of the whole, not as isolated stars.
Perhaps that is the secret of the orchestra's success.'

3.5   A Gentle but Persistent Character

In comparison with Karajan in his later years who had a
smaller and less solid figure, the orchestra acquired with
Abbado an extremely easygoing maestro for whom pressure
and haste were abhorrent. He was open to everyone,

Figure 3.2   Autograph seekers after an open rehearsal with Claudio Abbado.

always friendly and approachable. Many members of the Philharmonic got on well with him and appreciated his relaxed manner, which they interpreted as introverted and reserved. However, at the beginning of his appointment there were some musicians who took advantage of his pleasant bearing by concentrating less carefully at rehearsals or spreading commotion not very helpful for the common task. Sometimes, harmonious persons have difficulty in positions of leadership in an extremely self-aware collective ensemble.[3]

However, Abbado understood how to avoid conflicts. For him music alone stood front and center, so that personal quarrels between him and some members of the orchestra became insignificant. He was able in this way to lead the musicians gently yet with determination by a long leash. That is, whenever a member of the Philharmonic had a different opinion from his, he would politely request the other to reconsider the criticism, since nothing was further from Abbado's mind than insulting or putting someone in the wrong. But with trust in his intuition and with clever diplomacy and a smile, he usually had his way in the end - unless, insofar as the music was concerned, the other opinion proved to be superior.

Moreover, Abbado's personal staff relieved him of many things that might have been conflictual. This included bureaucratic decisions and press affairs as well as tasks Karajan had chosen to take over. Abbado did not direct operas but only conducted them, and at recording sessions he generally did not interfere with technical operations.

In any event, he succeeded in a short while to calm restlessness and meanwhile to arouse the evident enthusiasm of orchestra members for his way of interpretating music. Eventually, the orchestra became more versatile and flexible than in the final years with Karajan.

3.6 A View Inside

Abbado's reflective manner and his self-assurance meant that he made few comments during rehearsals and instead had passages played again and again with quiet elegance, so that the more subtle nuances were gradually absorbed. Occasionally he studied the score at length during rehearsals and made notes on matters that arose during practice sessions (in the presence of others Karajan never made notations on the score or studied it). As a rule Abbado approached a work slowly and, as he said himself, took his time to understand it completely.

He thus seemed to intuite a composition in order to find expressions that could release a sense of discovery in the audience. When everything was taken into account, he attained such a firm overview of the phrasing, dynamics, and dramatics of a piece that he was able to convey his feeling very effectively. Musicians with long experience in the orchestra said that he resembled in this regard Furtwängler, who likewise quietly accomplished his task.

In answer to my question about what moment in his profession he most appreciated, Abbado answered without hesitation: 'The quiet after the final note. Altogether the quiet is something very interesting, not only after the end of a concert or between movements, but also the quiet between humans.' More than through spoken words, he recognized the psychic condition of musicians through their slightest stir of emotion. One book on Abbado has the subtitle *Listen to the Others in Quiet*.[4] 'The vibrations in a room are important,' he said. 'Or the vibrations in nature'. Hence his love for the mountains.

Abbado's own gestures are symptomatic in this respect. At rehearsals he sometimes draws back from an all too loud tone as if it could injure him. Then he automatically slides his index finger to his pursed lips to indicate that the musicians should play more softly. In other situations he puts his extended hands together as in prayer, as if music had a sort of religious meaning for him.

3.7   Magically Transformed at Concerts

One of Abbado's characteristics was especially striking: his great charisma at performances. Then every member of the Philharmonic outdid himself and automatically gave his best to cope with his evident energy and decisiveness.

Abbado achieved this not only through a steady gaze, a pleading gesticulation, and a great ability to concentrate.

Figure 3.3 At concerts Claudio Abbado is especially charismatic.

In such moments he also had the unusual gift to create an overwhelming tension among everyone present. He combined the intensity of his own charisma with the capacity of the orchestra and somehow also the vibrations of the audience. At first, after most concerts, members of the Philharmonic, even the skeptical ones, looked at one another meaningfully as if they wanted to confirm that it had been correct to select Abbado as Karajan's successor. They knew then why he had made them practice again and again the details at rehearsals. Here was the real key to his success.

3.8   A Progressive Man

At rehearsals one difference with Karajan and others became apparent insofar as Abbado regarded every musician in the orchestra as a fully equal colleague.   He emphasized that everyone was to a considerable degree responsible for the interpretation of music. 'Each must play,' he said, 'as if the music were written only for his own instrument, with orchestral accompaniment.'

Abbado's attitude arises from his political conviction. Progressive thought is dear to him as with many of the 1968 generation and their supporters in Europe, especially in Berlin. His attitude was shared for many years with his communist oriented composer friend Luigi Nono, who died in 1990. Abbado admired both self-determination and tolerance, hoping thereby to bring persons of various origins, ages, ethnic groups, and religions together through music.

From this position some informal contact among members of the Philharmonic developed. For instance, Abbado supported common non-professional initiatives. He did not think it beneath his dignity to be a spectator at matches of the orchestra's soccer team, and he also took an interest in the musician's tennis and ping-pong tournaments.

Moreover, his invitation at the age of 59 that members of the Philharmonic, including the younger ones, should address him with his given name derived from his comradely comportment. This happened at a restaurant during a tour in Italy. It would have been unthinkable for Karajan to propose that he be called simply Herbert, and at that time no other great conductor had suggested such a thing to the Philharmonic. Most of the members were at least initially embarrassed, assuming that the familiar form might go too far (a 'Du' in the German language can easily become a sign of less respect, unlike the same form in other countries like Italy). In any case, each musician solved the problem in one way or another. Some - mostly the younger ones - addressed Abbado with 'Du'. Others avoided addressing him at all. And still others called him by first name while continuing the formal 'Sie'. In the meantime the usual practice with the current chief conductor Simon Rattle is the last of these.[5]

3.9   Programs with Thematic Framework

It was one of Abbado's major projects to collaborate
with various Berlin cultural institutions: theaters, cinemas,
galleries, museums, and literary establishments. After 1992
he instituted cycles with thematic fulcrums that embodied
his ideas. In May 1992 the theme was *Prometheus*; in the
following years *Hölderlin, Faust, Myths of Greek Antiquity,
Shakespeare, Berg and Büchner, The Traveler, Tristan and
Isolde, Music is Fun in the World*, and *Parsifal*.   Each
basic theme was presented through concerts, theater, dance
performances, films, bookreadings, lectures, or art exhibits.

In Abbado's book *Musica sopra Berlino*, he describes
how he had pursued the idea experimentally in Milan and
Vienna.[6] He wanted to create a cultural network through the
association of one theme in many fields of art, including music,
thereby showing that over centuries Europe communicated
basic values that would create a better world during many
generations. Not only through music, but also through words,
pictures, and dance, this could be repeatedly achieved. His
cycles were a fundamental contribution to the civilized world
and therewith a reminder of the tradition and cultural identity
of Europeans.[7]

In an interview Abbado explained that in a stage of
preparation he had attempted with the chief administrators
of the Philharmonic, first Ulrich Meyer-Schoellkopf and later
Elmar Weingarten, to discover where a given theme had left
traces behind. 'For the theme of antiquity we found nearly
a thousand titles, of which many had often been treated
musically. It is worthwhile to mobilize such interdisciplinary
initiatives,' he said, 'even when financing them is uncertain.
Young people learn mostly through associations.' In Salzburg
and Ferrara Abbado had organized similar forms of cultural
life.

3.10   A Classically Educated Maestro

Abbado's broadly based education in literary and artistic fields is legendary. 'I need reading for my inner balance', he once said. The maestro maintains contact with authors and writes or promotes books himself. His children's book *La casa dei suoni* (*The House of Sounds*) has been well received.

When rehearsing musical works closely related to literary themes, such as Verdi's *Don Carlos*, the original text lies next to the score - in this case Friedrich Schiller's play. Thereby he can offer the musicians tips about the literary context of a piece, and he mostly does so in their native tongue, since he not only speaks fluent English but also German, French, Spanish, and of course Italian.

3.11   Often on Tour

After the orchestra had been less often travelling with Karajan in the years preceeding his death, with Abbado's engagement a time began again in which the artistic director accompanied the orchestra on trips.[8] Naturally Abbado's native Italy stood on the program several times, but also distant lands like Japan and the United States. For the Philharmonic families it was not easy to have their fathers or mothers so often and so long underway. If one chooses randomly a certain period of time, for example May 1991 to October 1993, one must note 18 trips to 36 cities (see the graph on p. 156).

In Italy Abbado saw to it - much like Karajan earlier in Austria - that a festival center was developed at one place for a specific time of each year. That place was the university town of Ferrara, in the eastern Po Valley, for which Abbado (like Karajan for Salzburg) actively compaigned. Numerous cultural events were promoted by him there, with musical participations organized by the agency 'Ferrara Musica'. The price of tickets became just as expensive as in Salzburg.

3.12   A Reserved Private Life

For a long time it was unknown that Abbado's daughter Alessandra belonged to the 'Ferrara Musica' agency, since the maestro was always very discret about his private life - in contrast to Karajan who seldom avoided journalists. Abbado withdrew as if shocked whenever strangers asked for details. When the question was posed, after his engagement with the Philharmonic, whether he intended to move to Berlin, he answered: 'I have an inner residence'. Actually he did not live like Karajan solely in a hotel but had a private 'refuge under the roofs of the city'.

Photos of Abbado with his son Sebastian (an archeologist) from his first marriage and with his son Daniele (a movie director) from his second were much less frequently published than those of Karajan and his children. Most members of the Philharmonic did not know that his maternal grandfather, a professor of ancient languages in Sicily, had studied in Leipzig, or that his paternal grandfather had on occasion appeared as a conductor.

3.13   Many Honors

Through the years Abbado was a frequent recipient of awards (for example the *Großes Verdienstkreuz* of the German Federal Republic, three honorary doctorates, the honorary citizenship of several cities, the Ernst von Siemens music prize, the Edison Prize, a number of Grammys, and so forth), several of them for his conducting of the Berlin Philharmonic. With the orchestra he recorded - often thought unsurpassed in quality - all of Brahms's symphonies, and also works of Mozart, Mahler, Tchaikovsky, Prokofiev, Mussorgski, Dvořák, Hindemith, and Rossini. Yet he never became a media star to the extent of Karajan.

Some of his honors were received for his serious participation with youth orchestras, e.g., the Würth prize of the 'Jeunesses Musicales' of Germany or the golden medal of the international Gustav Mahler Society. Already in 1976 Abbado was active in founding the European Community Youth Orchestra (ECYO), whose musical director he remained for many years. In 1986, he helped to create the Gustav Mahler Youth Orchestra that brought many young talents from the East over the Iron Curtain.[9] He also encouraged artists graduating from youth orchestras to enter the Chamber Orchestra of Europe or the Mahler Chamber Orchestra, which were likewise founded with his help.

Since 1992, at the beginning of the yearly Berlin Festival, he brought youthful players together with experienced musicians. At these meetings he shared his abilities with young and old alike. In Salzburg he also sponsored competitions for composition, visual art, and literature for persons under forty. Prizes were offered through the Nonino family (known for its brand of grappa) and for graphic arts through the widow Eliette von Karajan.

3.14 Abbado Leaves Berlin

Everyone was astonished when Abbado announced in February 1998 that he did not wish to renew his contract as artistic director of the orchestra after the 2001/2002 season. It may be that press criticism contributed to this decision, but perhaps he had long considered it. Later the public learned that Abbado was suffering from stomach cancer. He was nonetheless able to muster enough strength to endure the stress of an already planned tour to Japan. In 2002 he also successfully led a so called 'Europe Concert' of the Berlin Philharmonic at Palermo. During these months his relationship with the orchestra became closer. In February 2002, when approached after a rehearsal at the Philharmonic,

Figure 3.4 Israel in 1993: Schönberg's *A Survivor of Warsaw*, with Claudio Abbado and the actor Maximilian Schell.

he said that it was the music itself that had aided his recovery: 'Through music you can gain everything, a good atmosphere in the orchestra and also personal health. It is the best relaxation. With music you can best overcome the moods and storms of life.' He executed his programs with an iron discipline and sought to direct the musicians as before. Even in rehearsals one could observe how - instead of withdrawing during pauses - he consulted with musicians as before and allowed himself only a few minutes of rest. His smile was now more serene than in earlier years. The thematic framework of Abbado's penultimate season as artistic director in Berlin was also the maestro's motto: *Music is Fun in the World.* As an optimist, even in the most difficult situations, Abbado chose this theme in reference to a closing sentence in Verdi's *Falstaff*: 'Tutto nel mondo è burla.' - *Everything is Fun in the World.* It may serve as his epitaph.

'One is not at home where he has an address but where he is understood.' (Christian Morgenstern)

4

The Orchestra on Tour

'The musicians are underway,' it is frequently said when visitors to Berlin ask about the Philharmonic. The orchestra has appeared with some chief conductors more often in other cities and countries than in Berlin, much to the pleasure of music lovers throughout the world.[1] It is thus able to perform live what the public only knows through records. Travel in a group usually creates both a sense of openness and community - and it also motivates the excellence of many members of the orchestra.

4.1   Travel Soon After the Founding

Concert tours have occurred since the founding year of 1882. At first they were a financial necessity in order to increase the modest salaries of the musicians. Alone in the first year the Philharmonic traveled to 24 German cities. Starting in 1885 it moved annually for four months to the Dutch coastal resort of Scheveningen - and did so for 26 years. Since 1890 the orchestra has continued guest performances also at other European locations, usually in the autumn and spring.

Until the middle of the twentieth century tours to distant cities were extremely strenuous. They became frequent with the introduction of air travel for tourists since the end of the

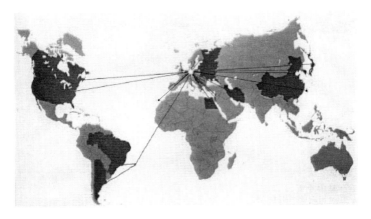

Figure 4.1 Tours of the Berlin Philharmonic outside Europe, 1882 to 2009.

1940s, and more so with jet airplanes since the 1960s. But still today foreign concerts are exhausting because of a crowded program.

4.2 Who and What Go Along

In the years when airplanes were ordinarily smaller, it was necessary to book seats in several planes. Besides the 129 regular members of the Philharmonic plus its conductor, there are usually substitutes to carry, not to mention staff members of the management such as the chief administrator and the head of the press department, plus technicians who arrange for transporting most of the instruments and set up the podium and the music literature once arrived. Many tours are accompanied by a travel guide, a physician, and an insurance representative (who watches over valuable instruments), and finally - depending on the importance and length of the trip - journalists, politicians, family members, and sometimes fans from home who want to experience 'their' orchestra for once elsewhere.

The luggage is considerable. Besides hundreds of suitcases and bags, it consists also of wooden and metal crates. Alone for the tuxedos for evening concerts and black suits for matinees, plus shirts and shoes, 65 huge boxes need to be carried, as well as cartons for scores. Packed instruments take the most space. Six or seven large crates are required solely for the violins and violas, since each holds only about ten instruments. The containers for harps, drums, cellos, and bass strings are of course huge. Depending on the destination and route, this freight (about 140 crates in all) flies in an air conditioned section in the hold of airplanes, or sometimes in a separate freight aircraft, if not transported by ship, train, or truck.

Some musicians take their instruments along in the cabin of the plane, such as the owners of valuable violins. The temperature in freight compartments could cause an extreme stretch of strings and an irreparable crack in the wood, and naturally there is a danger that instruments are somehow mislaid. The wish of cellists or bass players to maintain constant control of their instruments can only be satisfied by booking an extra seat for their treasures. Another reason for some musicians to keep their instruments with them in the cabin is a chamber concert before the beginning of the actual main performance.

Many members of the orchestra look on anxiously as the crates are unpacked in foreign concert halls. Has their instrument been damaged?

4.3   Destinations Today: in General

Most destinations lie in Europe, North America, and Japan, where the Berlin Philharmonic has its extremely loyal fans. Some other destinations, often discussed, have not yet been reached either because suitable concert halls were unavailable or financial arrangements lacking.[2] Plans must be settled three or four years ahead, and guarantees for the high costs cannot be given so long in advance in some countries with inflation.

Sometimes the orchestra nonetheless reaches unaccustomed places. It flew to Egypt in 1951, to Libanon in 1968, to Iran in 1975, to Communist China in 1979 (and again in 2005), to Korea in 1984 (and also in 2008), and to Israel for the first time in 1990. Finally the Philharmonic made a debut in South America (Argentina and Brazil) in 2000, in Taiwan in 2005 (portrayed in the film *Trip to Asia*), in the Canary Islands in 2006, and in the Baltic countries Lithuania and Estonia in 2008. Usually big cities are programmed, but also smaller towns in which a warmer reception is not infrequent. Karajan did not enjoy excursions of the whole ensemble into the provinces, believing that auditoriums there were not suited for a grand appearance.

Guest concerts are often combined with encounters with leading representatives of politics, culture, and business. From the end of the Second World War until 1989 that was especially important for musicians from Berlin. Above all, travels to the nations of the four occupying powers had political impact. Many an officer or soldier once stationed in West Berlin had visited the Philharmonic and then shared his enthusiasm for it back home. Hence the orchestra undertook several tours in Great Britain, France, and the United States. And even for Russia it repeatedly applied for entrance visas in order to be ambassadors of the West.

4.4 Europe

4.4.1 Great Britain

The orchestra had already appeared in London with Furtwängler in 1927. After the Second World War, in

Figure 4.2 A transport airplane loaded with the orchestra's luggage and the instruments after arriving at their destination (here still unpacked in Madrid). On the right the church of the cloister of Escorial.

November 1948, it arranged its first trip there. That was during the Berlin blockade, when the only possibility was to fly in military aircraft. Since West Berlin was at that time only lighted a few hours a day, members of the Philharmonic found less damaged London to be a metropolis from another world.

In 1949 and 1955 the Philharmonic appeared at the Edinburgh Festival. The 1955 trip, with guest conductors Ormandy, Sawallisch, Hindemith, and Keilberth, seemed at first quite problematic. The bass string player Friedrich Witt recalls with horror how two orchestra assistants, traveling with the instruments on the old freight double-decker *Queen Elisabeth*, reported that one motor stopped right in the middle of the English channel and that a second began to sputter. The pilot speculated about throwing the crates with the instruments as ballast overboard, but the precious weight was finally saved by landing at a nearby military base.

In June 1962 the Philharmonic undertook an impressive tour of reconciliation to Coventry to celebrate the reconstruction of the cathedral damaged in the Second World War. A few months before, Benjamin Britten had composed his *War Requiem*, which was performed on two evenings under the direction of Sir John Barbirolli and Eugen Jochum. Young persons were particularly invited to attend the overflowing church. In numerous speeches the gospel of Christian forgiveness was emphasized with pleas for grace and humanity. And in fact friendly relations were established between the musicians and the English families with whom they were lodged.

Since then several concert tours have visited English cities like Oxford, Manchester, and Birmingham. Also, since 1991, the orchestra has often participated in Prom-Concerts at the Royal Albert Hall in London, where a knowledgeable public is always in attendance.

4.4.2 France

The contact with France predates that with England, going back to 1897 when Arthur Nikisch traveled to Paris with the Philharmonic. After the Second World War, however, France was booked later than England on the orchestra's program. In 1950 it went to Paris and in the years following also to the French provinces. On one occasion a chamber concert group had an auto accident in southern France in which two members were killed and one severely injured.

At the beginning of the 1970s the orchestra was less often in France because Karajan - who had succeeded Charles Munch at the Orchestre de Paris in July 1969 - renounced his contract there in 1971. He was heavily engaged in Berlin and considered his increased presence in Paris to be no longer feasible.

In the two decades before the end of the century the orchestra made repeated guest appearances in Paris with Daniel Barenboim and Claudio Abbado. The press was full of praise, such as among others *Le Monde* (on 10 February 1993), which wrote: 'It is euphoric how the violins never lost their shading when they ranged from a deep *pianissimo* to a high *fortissimo*. Altogether the orchestra seems to have discovered a source of boundless energy.' The participation of Simon Rattle and the musicians at the festival in Aix-en-Provence since 2005 also receives each year enthusiastic praise in the media.

Of the many trips to France, one was to Versailles in the framework of the so-called *Europe Concerts* - not to be confused with the *Europe Tours* to many European countries. *Europe Concerts* are performed each year to one architecturally and historically significant site in Europe.[3] The Philharmonic chose May Day for this occasion because the orchestra was founded on the first of May 1882 and because the date marks a holiday in many countries so that people have the leisure for a concert. It first took place in 1991 when East and West Germany were about to become one Republic and when many were enthusiastic about the idea of a unified Europe. All performances are broadcast on radio and television in more than thirty nations.

In Versailles, the administrators of the monuments in France first did not give permission for a performance because the wooden structure of the Théâtre de l'Opéra Royal, an architectural masterpiece decorated in blue, red, and gold, can easily burn. Only after intervention of French President Jacques Chirac was it possible to make an exception.

On some occasions, trips to France are organized so that stops are possible in Brussels at the Palais des Beaux-Arts or in Amsterdam at the Concertgebouw.

4.4.3 Russia and Other European States of the East

Before the fall of the Berlin Wall the orchestra needed special permission for concert tours to Russia and other states in the East. The officials in West Berlin placed importance precisely on these contacts in order to allay resentments - despite the circumstances and the refusal of visas for some musicians. To avoid the East Berlin airfield Schönefeld, whence flights departed directly to Moscow or Leningrad, the orchestra flew from Berlin-Tempelhof or Berlin-Tegel to Russia via cities like Prague, Paris, or London, and returned by a similar route. These flights were always arranged with foreign airway companies, since aircraft of West German companies were not permitted to cross airspace of the German Democratic Republic (DDR).

Members of the Philharmonic valued trips to eastern block states at that time for the rare opportunity to become acquainted with the performance facilities there: for example, the imposing Kirov Theater in Leningrad (now St. Petersburgh) in which the Berliners appeared in May 1969 (later also in December 1991 and at a *Europe Concert* in 1996). Outside, the copper-domed building near the conservatory is magnificent, and inside the elegance and luxury of the Tsars is recalled by crystal chandeliers, gold trimming, priceless mirrors, and satin seats throughout the five decks. After Tsar Alexander II had in 1860 presented the house to his wife Maria - hence the longstanding name Mariinskij Theater - it was considered the most beautiful such edifice in Russia. From 1935 to 1992 it was baptized with the name of Sergey Kirov, the first Communist party secretary of the city, murdered in 1935.

Many music experts generally fill the audience of the Tchaikovsky Hall of the Moscow Conservatory. In May 1969, members of the Berlin Philharmonic were able to meet there Dmitri Shostakovich, who attended a performance of his *Tenth Symphony*, on which the musicians had worked hard. At the conclusion, the otherwise shy composer approached the podium, embraced Karajan, and said with tears in his eyes: 'I have never heard this composition so beautifully played.' The Iron Curtain seemed for an instant to part.

The hosts in some eastern block countries cleverly succeeded in hiding the rough edges of their political regimes. The orchestra performed in Prague in 1966, 1969, 1976, and 1991. In April 1997 it was in Sarajevo to collect funds for refugees from Yugoslavian war zones. When the musicians first appeared in the DDR at Dresden and Leipzig in 1978, they felt like citizens of an enemy state while presenting their West German credentials at the border. Three years later they gave another concert in the DDR, this time solely in Leipzig for the opening of the new 'Gewandhaus'. And finally, a half year before the fall of the Berlin Wall, James Levine conducted the orchestra in East Berlin (see p. 5).

4.4.4 Greece

In addition to countries occupying Berlin after the War, there were also tours that went to lands having extremely suffered under the Hitler regime. In the initial years after 1945, the Greeks responded very coolly to German visitors. Only gradually did their legendary hospitality revive toward Germans.

An important event in this regard was a music festival in Athens in the 1960s, during which the Berlin Philharmonic played several years in a row at the foot of the Acropolis in the open-air theater of Herodes-Atticus, with more than 5 000 spectators. It was rumored that Karajan's origins helped to obtain the first invitation (his ancestors were Greeks from Macedonia).

Once in the late summer of 1965 the orchestra combined its trip to Athens with an appearance in the vicinity at the amphitheater of Epidauros, about fifty miles away.[4] This antique monument from the 3rd century B.C., with seats for 14 000 spectators, was only fully restored in the 1950s. The Berlin Philharmonic was among the first non-Greek musicial groups permitted to perform there. Karajan was actually not enthusiastic about the invitation, since he usually was anxious about conducting outdoors. The music might disappear into air, and the chirping of crickets did not please him either. But nothing stirred on that evening in Epidauros. The marble bleachers of the theater were filled, the acoustics and atmosphere perfect. 'Even Verdi would have counted this

Figure 4.3 The Berlin Philharmonic in the ancient Herodes-Atticus amphitheater in Athens. The excellent acoustics and the view of the Acropolis make each of their concerts there an outstanding experience.

Sunday evening performance of his *Requiem* perhaps as one of his most memorable experiences,' wrote the London *Times* on 17 September 1965. The sky was black velvet, without a breeze. And as the moon appeared toward the concert's end, everyone was carried away by romantic feelings. Still today some members of the Philharmonic remember how they sensed the roots of western civilization on that evening.

4.4.5 Austria, Spain, Switzerland

Concerts with primarily natural lighting like Epidauros are exceptional for most musicians. Normally, although that is probably no issue for a music student in the choice of his profession, they are held under artificial light. The majority of concert and rehearsal halls have no windows, so that players are usually pleased to see daylight again. A praiseworthy exception in Vienna is the Golden Hall of the 'Verein der

Wiener Musikfreunde', which is also aesthetically notable for
its ceiling panels and the 32 gold-plated columns supporting
the balconies. Above all, the acoustics are excellent.[5]

Figure 4.4   The orchestra at rehearsal in Vienna's 'Musikvereinssaal',
one of the few concert halls with windows. Left, the oboist Albrecht
Mayer (l.) and Claudio Abbado; right, the violinist Stephan Schulze.

Naturally the acoustics in a concert hall are even more
important than the lighting. On tour, the musicians can
often have surprises. They therefore find rehearsals important
during which the conductor goes to the back of the auditorium
while the ensemble continues to play without his direction.
Ideally the sound is everywhere precise, full, and warm,
without echo even in fortissimo, thus transparent and not
blurred. Eugen Jochum roamed about Vienna's 'Golden Hall'
without ceasing to conduct, even though no one was watching
him, which provoked a few grins.

There are concert halls that swallow the music, so
that the orchestra must play loudly to be heard by the
audience in the back rows. Others are hyperacoustic,
that is, the notes resound harshly, requiring a softer tone,
often the case in churches. In Spain, for example, the
orchestra appeared in 1992 at the cathedral of Seville and

the cloister church of the Escorial, 40 miles northwest of Madrid. Especially in the latter instance the music during the *Europe Concert* of May first sounded very loud. Fortunately, through modern reproduction technique, listeners on radio and television noticed nothing awry. Inside, the concertgoers were compensated by the marvelous ninety-foot altar and the outstanding interpretation of the music with tenor Placido Domingo.

Whenever a hall is hyperacoustic, the orchestra's managers or conductors have organized drapes or curtains to moderate the tone. But that is often an insufficient solution to the problem, especially when loud pieces are on the program. Some passages become almost unbearable, for instance when the horns and woodwinds supported by drums are turned loose. In Alban Berg's *Three Orchestra Pieces* it in fact happened that a player who struck a wooden block with a mallet managed to splinter it. If in addition the air conditioning of a concert hall is inadequate, so that the musicians become bathed in sweat, they pine for the paradise of their music hall in Berlin.

For many years that was the case in Lucerne's old 'Kunsthaus'. The Berlin Philharmonic appeared there annually after 1958 for the International Music Festival Week (except in 1960, 1984, 2006, and 2009). Once a violinist helped Karajan down some steep stairs after an Alban Berg concert and asked the maestro how he found the performance. 'Plenty of noise!', was his biting response. Karajan and several local politicians pleaded for a new building, but the majority, especially in the ranks of the Swiss Labor Party, repeatedly declined. Finally, in 1998, the old house was replaced by an inspired new cultural center, designed by Jean Nouvel.

As a rule, the orchestra moves to Lucerne after the Salzburg Festival at the end of August, flying from Salzburg to Zurich, then moving by bus to Lucerne, an hour and a half away. The visitors from the North usually love the enchanting

mountain landscape on the Vierwaldstätter See, especially the
beautifully situated restaurants with a view over the lake and
the opportunities for boat and hiking trips.

In Switzerland there are of course also many concert halls
and churches with outstanding acoustics, as in Bern or Geneva
or smaller cities like Saint Moritz. In Saint Moritz Karajan
appeared with only a few members of the orchestra from 1964
to 1973, that is, in the years before founding the Salzburg
Whitsun Concerts. He had received as a present a parcel
of land to build a house there with the proviso that he offer
an evening concert each year. At first, recording sessions were
held in a small church. Later the promised concerts followed in
the Queen Victoria Hall or in Bad Saint Moritz (recordings of
five of the six *Brandenburg Concertos* as well as Bach's second
and third orchestral suites come from Saint Moritz). It was a
mixture of paid summer vacation and enjoyable music playing,
allowing Karajan to spoil the Philharmonic a bit, since the
remuneration was good and the first-class travel arrangements
went without saying. The maestro also arranged free rail
passes for everyone, including relatives, and invited them in
the name of the recording company to the best restaurants.
The violinist Hellmut Stern has described how the musicians
wrestled for the honor to appear in Saint Moritz.[6]

4.4.6 Italy

Naturally Italy also stood on the program. When Abbado
was chief conductor, such invitations became routine through
his close social relations to the Italian music world. The
orchestra traveled to Rome - performing in the concert hall
of the Academy of Santa Cecilia, one of Europe's eldest
musical institutions - and also to other cities (Milan, Turin,
Brescia, Ravenna, Reggio Emilia, Florence, Naples, Palermo,
and Ferrara - see p. 56), where they often played in beautiful
old theaters. Karajan had conducted years before in Venice's
Palace of the Doges, but later that was forbidden because of

fears that the ceiling of the great hall might be damaged by
vibrations.

The Italian press was always filled with praise. In
February 1993 *La Repubblica* noted that the violins sounded
like 'a single instrument', and *Il Messagero* said it was 'an
orchestra of pure delight'. The audiences sometimes threw
flowers at the conclusion of a concert. An international
club of fans, the 'Abbadiani', was established at that
time, documenting every detail of the maestro's career and
encouraging the orchestra to appear more often in Italy.[7]
That suited some of the musicians quite well, since they could
extend some concert tours a few days for vacations on the
Mediterranean or in Tuscany. For Abbado the favorite place
for relaxation was his farmhouse in Sardinia.

On 1 May 1995 a *Europe Concert* was held in the 'Salone
dei Cinquecenti' of the old city hall in Florence, which was
broadcast even to China, Japan, Korea, Mexico, the United
States, and South Africa. Soloist for the evening was 14 year-
old Sarah Chang, according to Yehudi Menuhin 'the most
wonderful, most perfect, and most accomplished violinist'
that he had ever heard.[8] Television viewers were given a
history lesson during intermission, learning that Michelangelo
and Leonardo da Vinci had designed this performance hall
and that the allegories portrayed on the ceiling and walls
documented the creation of one of the earliest republics in
Europe. These paintings found a perfect musical counterpart
in Beethoven's overture to *Fidelio* and the clashing tones of
Blacher's *Variations on a Theme by Paganini*.

4.4.7 Germany

It would be too much to enter into the details of all orchestra
tours. Yet, in closing this treatment of Europe, we may add a
few words about trips inside Germany, in former years mostly
executed by a special train organized for the musicians. For
decades a concert agency in the Ruhr was responsible for

these, led by the good humor and cleverness of Erich Berry. After the arrival in a given city he invited the musicians before the concert to a hearty meal, a custom dating back to the immediate postwar period when he assumed it was proper to stoke up the men prior to a performance. Erich Berry - and later his son Heinz - also had a small booklet printed before each trip with the expected dates and places, so that the way to the concert house, such as the hall on the 'Gasteig' in Munich or the 'Gürzenich' in Cologne, would present no problem.

In Wolfsburg the orchestra played ordinarily in the Volkswagen concert hall. When the musicians arrived on the railway station of Wolfsburg in October 1988, the VW band greeted them with a song, and then their leader asked the current conductor of the Philharmonic to direct his musicians. But Bernard Haitink, a somewhat introverted personality, was already deep in thought about a rehearsal for which little time was left and which was to be held in a hall unknown to him. He therefore refused with a smile despite encouraging calls from members of the Philharmonic. At the orchestra's departure, the band was there again, striking up a chorus of *Muß' i denn zum Städtele hinaus.*

In the small town of Meiningen in Thuringia the orchestra gave a *Europe Concert* on 1 May 1994 in the old court theater, which testified by its size to the former cultural importance of this place, which today counts only 22 000 residents. Meiningen was chosen because of the hundreth anniversary of the death of Hans von Bülow, as mentioned one of the first chief conductors of the orchestra (see p. 17). He had before his engagement in Berlin formed the court orchestra of Meiningen into a well regarded musical ensemble. During his six year tenure in Berlin (1887-93) he succeeded to lay the foundation of that extraordinary musical culture which the Berlin Philharmonic embodies.[9]

Figure 4.5 The concert hall of the small Saxon town of Meiningen, where Hans von Bülow worked very successfully. He was one of the first artistic directors of the Berlin Philharmonic. On the right, the musicians Bernd Gellermann (l.), Wolfgang Herzfeld (middle), and Peter Herrmann in front of the Brahms statue in Meiningen.

Some trips went to German cities in which Karajan had for many years occupied a leading position. When visiting in Ulm and Aachen he would wander to his old haunts, showing his wife Eliette and others the buildings where he had resided. 'In retrospect,' he once said, 'the old theaters in which I appeared seem much smaller than at that time.'

Members of the Philharmonic have a similar estrangement when it comes to distances because of the many miles they have traveled. So for some the long ways in the sprawling city of Berlin are no longer felt as long. If a musician lives in Berlin-Zehlendorf, for example like Rattle since 2008, he or she travels nearly a hundred miles in a single normal working day, most of the time without really noticing it: In the morning 10 to 25 miles to the Philharmonic building (despending on the location of their home in Berlin-Zehlendorf), then back again at noon, before returning in the afternoon for more rehearsals or in the evening to a concert, back and forth. By the time of retirement most of them, in distance, have circumnavigated the globe several times.

4.5   United States and Canada

The Berlin Philharmonic has also covered many miles in the last decades to guest appearances in the United States. Most of these trips, eight from 1955 to 2008, were undertaken during Karajan's time, sometimes accompanied by other conductors like Böhm and Jochum, who helped to manage the crowded program.   On two tours (1986 and 1991), Levine, Ozawa, and Haitink conducted. Others followed with Abbado (1993, 1996, 1998, and 2001), and with Rattle (several tours since November 2003).

At the beginning a reason for the frequent excursions to North America may have been Karajan's experience after Furtwängler's death in November 1954. As noted (p. 24) Karajan's career in Berlin began with the assignment of carrying out Furtwängler's already planned trip to the United States from February to April 1955. Concerts on the east coast were so successful that a second tour followed 18 months later to the Midwest and California, despite public agitation on the previous trip stirred by some immigrants from Nazi Germany.

In these initial years of worldwide tours the orchestra left from Berlin-Tempelhof in two small jet airplanes, requiring stops in Frankfurt or Düsseldorf, then in Iceland, the Azores, or Newfoundland and a flying time of some twenty hours. Later they departed in larger machines from Berlin-Tegel or Berlin-Schönefeld. To make these time-consuming trips worthwhile, the orchestra usually gave concerts in several cities, sometimes leaving no time for rehearsals.

During the 28 years that Berlin was enclosed by a wall and the USA was an occupying power, the vastness of America was hard for visitors from West Berlin to get used to. It happened one day that the orchestra played in one American town (Lafayette, Indiana) where the outside temperature was minus 25 centigrade and in another (Columbia, South Carolina) where it was plus 25 centigrade (77 degrees Fahrenheit). Travel arrangements did not always go as planned. One time a transport plane to Boston loaded with instruments and tuxedos had to turn around because of motor damage. A substitute plane arrived in such a rush that the instruments but not the tuxedos could be unloaded. Hence the Philharmonic appeared that evening in travel clothes. An oboe not yet accustomed to room temperature split open in the warmup.

Visits were of course connected with sight-seeing, above all in museums. After concerts in Washington D.C. orchestra members also visited the grave of John F. Kennedy; and in Huntsville, Alabama, they were all introduced to Wernher von Braun, who was then preparing the first landing on the moon. For a while, the Philharmonic appeared less often on the West Coast but did perform in 2003 in the newly inaugurated Walt Disney Hall in Los Angeles, the interior of which is partly inspired from the concert hall in Berlin. The poster with the announcement of the concert carried long in advance a banderole saying *Sold out.*

The orchestra also visited neighboring Canada, where it played in Toronto's Roy Thomson Hall, which can hold over 3 000 spectators, for Europe until recently an unusual number. Altogether there are in Canada and the US enormous concert halls, even in smaller cities like Lexington, Kentucky, with only a few hundred thousand residents (2 000-3 000 seats are not unusual; the Met in New York holds about 4 000). Yet the acoustics are excellent because these halls, like older large auditoriums in Europe, are built of wood with much space and swinging baffles for better sound, whereas in Europe new buildings are often constructed of cement and steel.

4.6   Japan

More often than in America the Berlin Philharmonic was in Japan, namely almost twenty times since 1957, offering more than a hundred concerts there even though in all only twenty to thirty concerts outside Berlin are programed per year.

Karajan was comfortable in Japan. He was enthused by the extraordinary respect for European classical music among Asians. Engaging local choruses with a specialty in German music proved to be no problem. He liked the politeness and attention of audiences and the Japanese facilities with new technology. Furthermore, he made numerous friends there, among others with the founder of the Sony concern, Norio Ohga.

In such distant lands it is essential in the first days for the musicians to overcome their jet lag. At the hotel, over breakfast or supper, impressions of the trip are discussed: taxi drivers wearing white gloves, window displays with plastic food in restaurants, school children's uniforms, or the many arcades with their noisesome play machines. The danger of earthquakes is of course also mentioned and the fact that the Japanese therefore install their skyscrapers on flexible rollers.

Some members of the Philharmonic use their time in Japan to appear before or after the actual concert with chamber orchestras, as did the *Twelve Cellists*, for instance in 1973 at the Waseda University. These occasions are often broadcast live on Japanese television, as are, of course, the full orchestra concerts. All categories of tickets are very expensive, about four times as much for the Berlin Philharmonic as for regular concerts.

Some musicians pursue their hobbies during their first days in Japan. Amateur photographers, for example, regularly visit the large specialized department stores for photographic materials in Tokyo. In some of them, on early morning, one can watch how the entire sales personnel goes through gymnastic exercises. Others use the opportunity to add some weird creatures to their butterfly or insect collection.[10]

Figure 4.6 One of eight street signs on a square in Tokyo.

In the 1970s and 1980s nearly every child in Tokyo recognized the last name of the chief conductor, though usually pronounced by them so it sounded to Western ears like 'Kalajan'. His recordings sold like hotcakes (and still break sales records today). A square in Tokyo is named after Karajan, in a complex of skyscrapers built by the soft drink concern Suntory, with towers, ponds, glockenspiel, and an elevated concert hall on Ark Hills. Viennese-style street signs with Karajan's name are scattered about the square.

After the performances, members of the Philharmonic are often asked about autographs, more in Japan than elsewhere. Young people stand for hours at the exit of the concert hall or in the hotel lobby. Once, as the musicians were being followed to their busses, a girl was injured as she attempted at the last instant to retrieve a signature through the window of a departing vehicle (her hand crushed against a cement pillar). The chief of the *Association of the Berlin Philharmonic* visited her later in the hospital, brought her flowers, the autographs of many of the orchestra's musicians, and their latest recording. In 2004, when the orchestra - together with Simon Rattle - visited Tokyo and also smaller cities like Kanazawa, and again in 2005 and 2008, such an incident fortunately did not recur.

Figure 4.7 On tour, many members of the orchestra use the occasion to perform in chamber groups (here the Horn Quintet on *Karajan Place* in Tokyo). On the right, the violinist Lutz Steiner walking on the Great Wall of China.

4.7 China

In October 1979, the orchestra added to its concert tour in Japan a trip to the People's Republic of China. This was one of the first attempts from the German side to establish contact with the country which had been isolated for a decade by the so-called Cultural Revolution. Mao Zedong had died three years earlier, and his successors were grasping for a way to the West by inviting table tennis or musical groups.

Because of the extended rupture, the Lufthansa asked cautiously whether the Beijing airport had landing platforms for its DC 10. If not, a folding ladder would have been brought from Germany. The Chinese assured that they would take care of it and did so. But the strength of the light metal contraption provided by them had been miscalculated. As the cellist Alexander Wedow and the oboe soloist Lothar Koch crossed the gangway, it broke in two and they fell about nineteen feet below. Both came with broken bones to a Beijing hospital before being flown back home.

Numerous diplomats and businessmen were of course present at concerts. At an elegant reception of the German Embassy one day, a young artist played a virtuoso performance of Sarasate's *Gypsy Ways* on a two-string knee violin. The accompanying feast was opulent, creating a favorable atmosphere for negotiations to inaugurate an economic exchange.

It goes without saying that the musicians also exploited their free time to explore this strange land. Especially impressive were the grey or blue uniforms typical at that time, the many military guards, the numerous bicycles, and the busy markets. Everyone wanted to see the Great Wall of China. For Berliners of that era a dividing wall was no novelty, except that this one was so wide that a hike on it was possible. Also unusual were the large crowds at morning rehearsals, attended as much as evening concerts by a public that did not cease to chatter unperturbed. For one rehearsal a meeting with the Beijing Symphony was arranged. The two orchestras practiced together and in the evening held a joint concert. Beethoven sounded weirdly Chinese to western ears.

In 1981, in response to this visit, for the first time musicians from the People's Republic were invited to Berlin: the conductor Huan Yijun, the composer Wu Tsu-Chiang, and the piccolo player Liu Teh-Hai. When the manager Peter Girth invited these guests to his home after the concert, the conductor - and former pianist - told him that all of his fingers had been broken during the Cultural Revolution and that he had been held prisoner for a long time in a cellar.

'In the meanwhile', wrote Eleonore Büning in the *Frankfurter Allgemeine Zeitung* on 10 January 2005, 'the young dynamic generation in China loves above all that which Mao once had damned.' Nowadays classical European music is praised by many Chinese as an instrument of modern education. The Berlin Philharmonic traveled a second time to China in 2005 to present with Simon Rattle a Richard Strauss program at the Beijing Music Festival under the title 'China and Germany'.

4.8   Iran

The orchestra was also in Iran for three concerts from 7 to 12 November 1975, for the opening of the great concert hall in Teheran - a very impressive occasion. Karajan was acquainted with the Shah of Persia and his wife Farah Diba from Saint Moritz, where they were next door neighbors on the Suvretta. The families often visited one another. Hence Eliette von Karajan and both daughters accompanied the maestro to Teheran. On a free day between concerts they also went along on a plane trip to the ancient Persian city of Isfahan, where they admired the beautiful blue mosque and the weaving of expensive rugs.

At the time Iran was a powderkeg. Already at the arrival the orchestra's airplane was carefully searched. Instruments were turned upside down, and the musicians had to half undress at the security check. The Shah's palace lay on a plateau from which a six-lane highway led to the concert hall. It was partially cordonned off to avoid any incidents.

In the concert hall the Shah was only briefly seen in his box behind a balustrade. At the second concert it happened that applause began before the end of the piece. The explanation was other than expected: loud trumpets and pounding drums toward the end of Richard Strauss' *Till Eulenspiegel* (as Till is led to the gallows) was understood as a signal that the Shah was entering and should be applauded.

4.9   Israel

One country in which the orchestra has likewise seldom played is Israel. True, already in 1965, after diplomatic relations between Israel and the Federal Republic of Germany were restored, sentiment gathered in the orchestra in favor of conducting a tour to Israel. But the Israel Philharmonic Orchestra, with which the decision about such an arrangement lay, was not in support. 'Maybe the Berliners, but without Karajan,' it was said in reference to the maestro's affiliation with the Nazi party from 1935 to 1942.[11] Out of solidarity with its chief conductor, the musicians declined, also in 1967, when the same proposal was made and refused again. Administrator Wolfgang Stresemann diplomatically announced that he felt the undertaking was premature in view of the experience of many Jews in Germany during the Hitler era.[12]

Instead of a tour to Israel, Jewish musicians were invited to Berlin. The Jewish pianist Daniel Barenboim and the Israel Philharmonic Orchestra with chief conductor Zubin Mehta (an Indian) performed Paul Hindemith's symphony *Mathis der Maler* at the Philharmonic hall in September 1965. And in 1967, as the Six Day War was underway in the Near East, the Israel Philharmonic staged a special concert of Beethoven's *Ninth Symphony* under the direction of Sir John Barbirolli, at the initiative of violinist Hellmut Stern, who held both German and Israeli citizenships.

Later, when Karajan, by then over 80 years old, failed to invite the Berlin Philharmonic in time to the Salzburg Easter Festival of 1990 - after 23 consecutive appearances in Salzburg - several members of the orchestra favored a trip to Israel that April instead. Besides concerts in Jerusalem and Haifa under the direction of Daniel Barenboim, joint performances with Israeli musicians in Tel Aviv were planned. The mayor of Berlin, Walter Momper, accompanied the Philharmonic.

As always on tour, the members again took the time to look about. One event is still mentioned by the musicians: at Yad Vashem, near Jerusalem, the tour guide proposed that the musicians purchase tiny trees to plant as a symbol to their attachment to Israel. Many followed this proposal in order to fortify German-Israeli friendship.

In 1993 a second visit took place on the fiftieth anniversary of the Warsaw Ghetto uprising. The performance of Schönberg's music was dramatically suited to awaken sinister memories. In the newspaper press it was said that deep feelings awakened by this presentation of the *Survivor of Warsaw*. Perhaps that success had to do with chief conductor Claudio Abbado, who wanted to deliver with the concert a moral and social message. Through the connection of his family to Jewish musicians during the Second World War, this voyage was a deeply emotional matter of reconciliation.

By now the orchestra has established very friendly relations with Israel. Since several years, an Israeli, Guy Braunstein, is one of the concert masters of the Philharmonic - which also has more than a dozen other nations represented in its ranks - and the growing number of Jewish musicians employed has increasingly enriched the orchestra.

'Conductors come and go, the orchestra remains'. (Wolfgang Stresemann)[1]

5

Guest Conductors

Guest conductors stand at the very top of persons important for the Berlin Philharmonic. In the last half century hundreds of guest conductors have appeared with the orchestra, of which two-thirds one to three times only, often initially as substitutes.[2] Seventy-two concerts were directed by them during the 2002/2003 season alone, by the chief conductor thirty-one.

Many guest conductors have introduced music not yet attempted. Others rendered such idiosyncratic interpretations of frequently played works that regular concertgoers were offered interesting comparisons. Following are comments on some of these personalities.

5.1   A Particular Case: Leonard Bernstein

Deserving special mention is the great New Yorker Leonard Bernstein. He left a very deep impression on the musicians even though he only prepared one work with them, Gustav Mahler's *Ninth Symphony*, at the Berlin Festival in the autumn of 1979. As so often when guest conductors are invited, the chief conductor at the time, Herbert von Karajan, was elsewhere occupied with other obligations. The two did not meet.[3]

Bernstein was accorded four rehearsals rather than the usual three. The musicians were surprised when he entered the hall: 'What a delicate person! How informally he is clad in a leather jacket, a bracelet, a striped T-shirt!' He held a cigarette package in his hand. No conductor had done so before, since it is forbidden to smoke in the concert hall, even at rehearsals.

It did not last long before the orchestra understood Bernstein's reputation. His great knowledge, charisma, and

Figure 5.1 Leonard Bernstein was the only guest conductor to smoke in the rehearsal room. Members of the Philharmonic experienced him in 1979 as American informality paired with the most intense concentration.

ingratiating presence captured everyone as soon as he began
to speak and wave his baton. Unlike most conductors he
first held a brief lecture on the meaning and content of the
composition at hand and explained it in simple terms with
seriousness and great philosophical grasp. Only then did he
turn to the score, a scene repeated in the second rehearsal.

The initial reserved skepticism of some members of the
Philharmonic soon dissipated through his almost fanatical
enthusiasm for music (at the podium he sometimes leaped into
the air), an optimism shared by the musicians as they left the
rehearsal hall. Not until the third session did the orchestra
concentrate totally on their instrumental part. Bernstein
helped with difficult passages, for example to bridge the
gap between inner tension and passionate expression. When
complicated pianissimi required long strokes of the bow for
violins in the midst of loud dramatic moments, he attempted
to calm the players: 'It's all in fun,' he said, 'all in fun!' (one
of his books is entitled *Fun in Music*). This was especially
refreshing because the nay-sayers had the upper hand in those
days in many social circles. After the performances on 4 and 5
October 1979 the musicians and the public were both uplifted
with a feeling that they had participated in a fabulous musical
event.[4]

5.2 The Honored Maestri Böhm, Jochum, and Giulini

Unlike Bernstein, other guest conductors appeared frequently
in Berlin, again and again offering their talent, pedagogical
ability, and large repertoire. From the 1920s to 1960, that is
decades before Karajan's engagement and in the first years
of his time in Berlin, such virtuoso conductors came as Carl
Schuricht, Ernest Ansermet, and Otto Klemperer. Great
impetus was also given by Sir John Barbirolli, usually on

concert tours, and George Szell, until 1970 during the annual tour to Lucerne.

Two conductors of an elder generation remained favorite guests into the 1980s: Karl Böhm and Eugen Jochum. Another, Carlo Maria Giulini, debuted only at the age of 53 with the Philharmonic, in October 1967, and reappeared until September 1992. Following are a few comments on these three conductors.

The always modest Karl Böhm (1894-1981) traveled from Graz to Berlin as guest conductor for 45 years, from 1935 to 1980. In rehearsal pauses there was much laughter, especially during Böhm's final two decades, because one musician learned to imitate his somewhat dry manners.[5] Like others of his age, Böhm preserved his energy while conducting by essentially moving only a single finger. Yet he was able to express the same atmosphere as others did with wild gestures. Perhaps he had observed this manner with his mentor, Richard Strauss, whose works he prepared with the orchestra (for example the *Symphonic Poems*). Franz Strauss, Richard's father, had once said to his son: 'It is unseemly when conducting ... to make movements like a snake.'[6] Böhm's worldwide reputation grew, especially as he became older. He was still conducting the Berlin Philharmonic at age 85. Shortly after Böhm's death at age 87, on 3 October 1980, the orchestra gave a concert of Mozart and Schubert in his honor - *without* a conductor.[7]

Equally important for the Philharmonic was Eugen Jochum (1902 - 1987), a product of the great German tradition of 'Kapellmeister'. He almost became Furtwängler's successor. At general rehearsals he would often say just before the end: 'Gentlemen, only a few small details.' He would then ask to replay an entire movement, so that the musicians could never be sure to return home on time. But everything should be perfect. It seemed as though the born Bavarian was virtually Prussian in his bearing. Because of his huge size - and later his head of white hair - he earned a number of nicknames like 'the German oak' or 'the white giant'. His interpretations of Bruckner symphonies are legendary.

Figure 5.2   Guest conductors of the older generation: Eugen Jochum and Carlo Maria Giulini.

As for the ascetic Carlo Maria Giulini (1914-2005), Karajan often repeated that he was one of the most cultivated and versatile conductors. When the tall slender man entered the hall, he did so with great dignity, approaching the concert master, shaking his hand, and greeting the musicians with a friendly smile. At rehearsals he then took off his cardigan, opened the score, and began to conduct with scarcely a word. He interrupted the piece only occasionally and gave little explanation, apparently having the gift of staring at each player so that he knew exactly how to perform. Impressive were his large smooth gestures and an expression reflecting his notion that art is always spiritual. Giulini made few enemies and was sensitive to social injustices. Some members of the Philharminc considered him a Renaissance man, whom Botticelli could have portrayed.

5.3   Some Possible Successors to Karajan

When it came to choosing a chief conductor after Karajan, the list of potential successors was secret, though several names

were obviously under discussion. Among them were Bernard
Haitink (born in 1929), Zubin Mehta (1936), Riccardo Muti
(1941), Carlos Kleiber (1930-2004), and Lorin Maazel (1930).
Claudio Abbado (born in 1933) joined this group as a surprise
candidate (see pp. 45-59). In addition, Karajan himself
mentioned a few colleagues: Giulini, who gratefully declined
because of his age, only six years Karajan's junior; Seiji
Ozawa, heavily engaged elsewhere, especially in the United
States and Japan; Mariss Jansons and James Levine, both
also engaged abroad; as well as Semyon Bychkov and Simon
Rattle, who were too young.[8] Let us comment on the first five.

The Dutchman Bernard Haitink started to conduct the
Philharmonic in 1964. Since then he has been very popular
with the orchestra because of his reliability, his even-tempered
manner, and his talent to organize tours. He often substituted
whenever the orchestra needed help, for instance in 1976 when
Karajan was indisposed by an operation, several times in the
1980s when Karajan appeared less frequently because of his
age, and also in the summer of 2000 when Abbado was ill. His
professional manner may strike an outsider as unemotional,
but members of the Philharmonic appreciate his passionate
involvement especially in the classic and romantic repertoire.
As a somewhat introverted personality, he did not want to

Figure 5.3 Guest conductor Bernard Haitink and Lorin Maazel, the last
with the singer Sarah Brightman (at the time married to the composer
Andrew Lloyd Webber).

waste words and occasionally used expressions like: 'That should sound like a cellar in the dark' or 'Think of a portrait of Rembrandt'. It may be that some orchestra members, in the choice of Karajan's successor, did not sufficiently appreciate his cautious manner (see p. 74). He went several times with the orchestra to the Salzburg Easter Festival and once in the summer to the United States.[9]

Also Zubin Mehta, a native of Bombay, always came gladly when invited by the Berlin Philharmonic. He is surely one of the most cosmopolitan conductors of all, educated in India, Austria, and Italy. He was artistic director in Montreal, Los Angeles, and New York, and is chief conductor for life of the Israel Philharmonic Orchestra. The music critic Karl Schumann has written that Mehta - whose father was founder of the Bombay Symphony Orchestra - gave a signal, even before Seiji Ozawa, that Asia was about to make an entrance in the concert halls and opera houses of the West. Mehta is a *Grandseigneur* with exotic fascination. His sense of humor, his strength, and his meditative spirituality became famous. With Karajan he got on well, and even better with Abbado, who was a fellow student in Vienna, where both were tutored by Hans Svarovsky.[10] The tonal elegance of his interpretations and the dramatic quality of his gestures are striking.

Riccardo Muti proved equally expressive as Mehta during his more than thirty years of association with the Berlin Philharmonic. Karajan thought of naming him 'Principal Guest Conductor' - along with Ozawa and Maazel - but this English system was finally not introduced to Berlin. Many members of the orchestra would gladly have seen the rational yet vital Italian named as Karajan's successor. The two in a certain way resembled each other in appearance and character - for instance, the aristocratic but at the same time athletic manner. Muti can be aimiable one minute and authoritarian the next. He is especially keen about fairness. Thus in 1982 he sent some musicians home from a recording session because they had participated neither in rehearsals nor performances of Verdi's *Quattro pezzi sacri*. Abbado's relations with Muti were regarded with amusement. For years the former considered his eight-year younger compatriot as his main competitor. When Abbado left the Scala in Milan in 1986, Muti became the chief musical director there. But shortly before the decision of the Berlin orchestra about Karajan's succession, Muti let it be known that he was unavailable.[11]

Besides the 'solid' maestros there are those who, at a tender age, had been child prodigies passing from podium to podium and thus skipping the years of labor in the provinces. Lorin Maazel was such a talent, as was also at a similar age the Berliner Carlos Kleiber, who only conducted the orchestra one time, on 9 March 1989, prior to the election of Karajan's succession. He withdrew from competition before an offer could be made.

Until the last minute the American Maazel was the favorite. He came from a successful musical family and appeared on stage with his violin while his classmates were learning their spelling. He made his debut as conductor at the age of nine, though he was 29 when he first directed the Berlin Philharmonic in January 1959. Starting in 1965 he was for ten years, next to Karajan, the star of classical music in Berlin, until 1971 as general music director of the Deutsche Oper and until 1975 also as chief conductor of the Radio Symphony Orchestra. Many considered Maazel to be the most genial of orchestra conductors, with his photographic memory of scores, his absolute tone pitch, and his elegantly precise baton technique. Others found, however, that after exploring the smallest detail at rehearsals, he would conduct indifferently at concerts as if the entire affair bored him.[12] With Abbado, who was finally chosen, such a critique was unthinkable.

5.4   Other Guest Conductors

Among musicians there are many stories about conductors. Beyond the usual gossip, some attempt is made to establish a certain pecking order in their description of the different personalities. The solo drummer Rainer Seegers has this to say: 'Fortunately there are many whose lives have not been too much affected despite managers and riches or fame and flattery. They seem less restless than others who constantly flutter between the big cities like Berlin, London, Vienna, Paris, or New York. They draw more attention to the musical works than to themselves, seldom stir a controversy, and are generally unconceited and usually also more satisfied. Many of them have a passion for teaching.' Seegers names among such personalities old masters like Wolfgang Sawallisch, Lovro von Matačić, André Previn, Sándor Végh, Nikolaus Harnoncourt, Rafael Frühbeck de Burgos, Hanns-Martin Schneidt, Klaus Tennstedt, and Gerd Albrecht. It was true of them all that they allowed themselves no extravagances or spectacular performances such as for instance, those of Hans von Bülow in the 19th century. He directed the funeral march from Beethoven's *Eroica* with black gloves (the other movements with white). He had the musicians remain standing throughout some concerts, and he sometimes presented the same piece twice in a performance. By comparison Furtwängler also belonged in a way to the more modest conductors and disdained colleagues who wallowed in narcissistic effects.

Seegers mentions two other conductors belonging among those without a nimbus of stardom: Günter Wand (born in 1912) and Erich Leinsdorf (1912-1993). They soberly regarded their profession as artisanal. Because of his Rhenish accent Wand was known as the 'Lad from Cologne', since he devoted himself for thirty years almost exclusively to the music life of Cologne and did not begin to frequent Berlin more often until he was in his seventies. His specialty was sacred music.

Leinsdorf also came late to Berlin as the orchestra's guest conductor, a consequence of his emigration from Austria during the Nazi period. He is remembered for saying: 'Everything can be conducted as a big whole', by which he justified his habit of raising his hand up and down but one time per beat, avoiding superfluous florishes. Seegers also notes that, with Leinsdorf conducting, the most complicated works seemed simple. He scarcely ever prolonged rehearsals beyond their alloted time even though he was an analytic perfectionist.

5.5 Two Special Conductors: Georg Solti and Seiji Ozawa

Among the guest conductors two stand out who were for a time of extraordinary importance for the orchestra. After Karajan's death, Georg Solti was for two years the artistic director of the Philharmonic at the annual Salzburg Easter Festival. Also Seiji Ozawa, a protégé and close friend of Karajan, often substituted for him, and after Karajan's death frequently appeared in Berlin. For their long aritistic and personal relationship with the orchestra, both received the Hans von Bülow medal.

Musicians say of the Hungarian-English guest conductor Solti (1912-1997), who debuted with the Berlin Philharmonic already in 1947, that he set extremely high standards for the players and managers. In his later years he lived by the principle that great accomplishments allow no compromises and that money plays no role. According to the music critic Jungheinrich, Solti seemed to be 'a determined authoritarian' and 'a completely dominating and temperamental musician' who tolerated no contradiction.[13] It therefore sometimes came to turbulent scenes. At the Bayreuth Festival, where some Berlin Philharmonic members also collaborated, he once wanted to replace horn players with some from his own orchestra in Chicago - which was naturally rejected as absurd and only excused by his impulsive nature. Solti has nonetheless entered history as one of the most decorated of conductors with more than thirty Grammys, many honorary doctorates, and the British aristocratic title of 'Sir'.

Figure 5.4 Left, guest conductor Georg Solti (r.) with bass soloist Friedrich Witt. Right, Seiji Ozawa.

Seiji Ozawa, whom Karajan took under his wing for several months after a debut in the Philharmonic on 21 September 1966, made the opposite impression. At least in a Western perspective, he is in his appearance the image of modesty and relaxed conducting. During performances he is often bent forward as if borne by waves of melody. Like Mehta he had to make a greater effort to gain recognition because he grew up far from the fount of classical music (born 1935 in Manchuria). During the 1960s, he was made the director of some orchestras in North America, and he has appeared on occasion with the Berlin Philharmonic since 1970 in Salzburg. He also accompanied the orchestra on several tours abroad, conducted it in 1982 during the Philharmonic's hundredth anniversary celebration, introduced various Japanese composers,[14] and led the orchestra two times (1993 and 2003) in front of 22 000 spectators at the *Berliner Waldbühne*. Karl Schumann has aptly characterized this agile Asian as the 'gyrating figure of a Javan dance puppet'.[15]

5.6 Composers Conduct their Own Works

To be emphazised among the numerous guest conductors are also composers who perform their own works.[16] Countless times in the past years the orchestra has hosted masters of avant-garde music such as Witold Lutoslawski, Karlheinz Stockhausen, Krzysztof Penderecki, Udo Zimmermann, Matthias Pintscher, Wolfgang Rihm, or the Chinese Tan Dun. Since the 1990s, some became composers-in-residence, that is, they were invited to Berlin to contribute to the musical programming. This idea originated during the stay of the Latvian Jewish composer Alfred Schnittke at the Berlin 'Wissenschaftskolleg'. Connaisseurs came to listen to such concert pieces.

Earlier, in the 19th century, it was common for conductors also to compose. The profession of being exclusively a conductor first arose as the repertoire became more extensive and the orchestras larger, so that pedagogical talents were required. It is known that Beethoven possessed little of that talent. The chief administrator Wolfgang Stresemann thought it ideal when composers take the baton and introduce their own personality. He wrote that the best music occurs when composers explain all details in rehearsals, including those that do not appear in the score.[17] Some composers visit the orchestra, however, just to observe how their works are performed. Good music, they say, permits various interpretations, and performances vary anyway in time through different tastes and social contexts.

An exciting experience for the orchestra since 1962 has been the repeated collaboration with Hans Werner Henze. He managed to arouse interest again and again, even among skeptics, by crossing the border of tonality. His initial rehearsals were usually a huge chaos, among other reasons because the scoring for some individual instruments was difficult to read. But after the musicians heard the piece for a while with the ears of its creator, no one ended up playing something that, at the outset, did not please him.[18]

The public reacted variously. In the 1960s such music struck some as the harbinger of a coming revolution, whereas others thought it too reactionary because it contained elements of earlier compositions (Henze, for example, loves Bach). And there are those who always reject concerts of this sort as unbearable. It does not suit their taste, for instance, to have excentric instrumentation with computers or special effects by placing musicians in the balcony, not to mention a mixture of classical and rock music, oriental sounds, atonal passages, or theatrical presentations by speakers, actors, and singers, with special costumes and decorations.

Figure 5.5 Carl Orff (l.) after a concert of his *Carmina Burana*, pictured here with the former concert master of the Berlin Philharmonic, Thomas Brandis. On the right, the composer Hans Werner Henze.

The greatest satisfaction for a composer, said Carl Orff (1895-1982), is to have his works remain in the program for a very long time.[19] This is the case for works of his younger colleague Pierre Boulez (born 1925), although - or because - a conservative philharmonic 'Gemütlichkeit' is lacking. Like many other living composers, his compositions are controversial, leaving behind a sour taste, according to the press, and sweeping cobwebs from the ear. Yet he has meanwhile become known even to persons who have never heard a note of his.

Sometimes these composer-conductors with the Berlin Philharmonic also present works of others. On such occasions they usually remain in the background, probably because they have more respect than others for the composition. But the attempt to avoid any arbitrary personal interpretation can also lead to somewhat dryer concerts.

The greatest tribute of a composer to an orchestra is when he dedicates a work to the entire organization and its chief conductor. That happened in 1994 when György Kurtág wrote a dedication on the score of his composition entitled *Stele*: 'For the Berlin Philharmonic and Claudio Abbado'.

5.7   Some Candidates to Succeed Abbado

After Abbado gave notification on 13 February 1998 that he would no longer be available as chief conductor after the 2001/2002 season, a successor was elected on 23 June 1999. One of the candidates was Daniel Barenboim (born in November 1942). Andrew Clarke reported in the London

Figure 5.6 Guest conductors Daniel Barenboim (l.) and Mariss Jansons.

Financial Times that in a preliminary vote Barenboim received 25 percent of the ballots, trailing Simon Rattle (born in January 1955) with 43 percent. However, only very few (a lawyer and some of the musicians and administrators) know whether those figures are correct.

Barenboim is admired not only because of his great musical ability but also his charm and his gentle sensitivity. He made an unusual entrant among conductors because he was at first mainly a star soloist, like the pianist-conductor Christoph Eschenbach, the violinist-conductor Yehudi Menuhin, and the cellist-conductor Mstislav Rostropovich. At an early age he gained his reputation as a boy prodigy on the piano, and thus appeared initially with the Berlin Philharmonic. That was in June 1964. Only five years later did he stand on the podium as conductor. His gestures made an effect: the widely stretched arms and the slightly bent upper torso.

Notable is Barenboim's generosity. Several times the members had the pleasure to share his refined life style, as in Paris and Seville, where he hosted them lavishly. Just as was the case for Karajan, after whose resignation in April 1989 he often appeared as guest conductor, his phenomenal memory is legendary (he conducts during concerts without a score). Similar to Abbado, whom he has known since childhood, his attempts to achieve cultural reconciliation through music are noteworthy. He has brought Germans and Israelis as well as Arabs and Jews together through joint performances (he is the founder of the West-Eastern-Divan-Orchestra, an annual meeting of young Jewish and Arab musicians since 1999).[20] When the Berlin Philharmonic appeared for the first time in Israel, he was its conductor (see p. 83). And later, despite protests in Israel, he was the one to put the composers Richard Wagner and Richard Strauss on the program there. In 1992 Barenboim became the artistic director of Berlin's State Opera Unter den Linden and he is also since 1991 director of the Chicago Symphony Orchestra.

In 1999, among the hotly debated candidates for chief conductor was, in addition, the Latvian Mariss Jansons (born in January 1943). After his education in Leningrad, he studied under Karajan in Salzburg, was engaged as artistic director of the Oslo Philharmonic in 1979, and became intermediately recognized through guest performances in Berlin, London, Saint Petersburg, and New York, as well as his stint with the Pittsburgh Symphony Orchestra. He has often been requested to base programs on his collaboration with Russian composers, which he has done with great success.

As the balloting came to a close however, the choice as Abbado's successor was decisive: the new chief conductor would be Simon Rattle.

Figure 5.7 Simon Rattle as guest conductor with the Philharmonic in a 1987 rehearsal of Gustav Mahler's _Sixth Symphony_. Before his appointment as chief conductor, he appeared 75 times with the orchestra.

5.8   Unaccustomed Guest Conductors

Conductors who appear for the first time before the orchestra take a different length of time until the musicians become accustomed to them, each according to his or her personality.

Whenever women take the conductor's podium, complex precedents are especially placed into question. Since its founding the Berlin Philharmonic has performed with less than ten female guest conductors,[21] of which only one during the seventy-eight years from 1930 to 2008, Sylvia Caduff, who substituted for Karajan during his illness on 15 October 1978. That occurred four years before the engagement of the first female member of the orchestra.

Tolerance was extended before the fall of the Berlin Wall also to lesser known Russian, Polish, Czech, Bulgarian, and even East German maestros. They were especially invited to West Berlin to maintain a bridge to the east through music and to counter the inertia of the political climate. For example, Juri Temirkanov, Valery Gergiev, and Emil Tchakarov came to West Berlin respectively in 1970, 1977, and 1979. In exchange, the orchestra hoped for an invitation from the Eastern block countries. This occasionally happened, for example when the newly restored concert hall 'Neues Gewandhaus' in Leipzig was opened in October 1981 and the very influential Kurt Masur obtained permission for the orchestra from West Berlin to play there in the series *International Orchestras.*

The concerts became more varied through East European conductors because, as Norman Lebrecht puts it, they had 'entirely their own style'.[22] But it was necessary for the musicians to become accustomed to them, also in non-musical regards. Scarcely any of them spoke fluent German - except of course citizens from East Germany - and their English was usually undeveloped. Moreover, one or another of them was seen with a glass of vodka in hand, not only after concerts. In many cases the guests did not display the casual manner with which, for instance, some American conductors presented themselves to the orchestra.

That included Kurt Masur, who first appeared with the Philharmonic in 1976. Some musicians thought he seemed very 'East German'. Karl Schumann describes him as a maestro from the puffed-up stolid Middle German school in which musicians ascended to the podium through endless repetitions and regularity.[23] Yet Karajan held him in high estime. In 1989 everyone was astonished by Masur's intervention in Leipzig in favor of the political change in East Germany. Since then he has become quite successful in the West.

Unaccustomed for some members of the Philharmonic were also guest conductors who were either all too elegant (for example, Christoph von Dohnányi) or all too boisterous (Horst Stein). Their comportment was to be explained in part by their biography. Dohnányi, for instance, comes from an old Hungarian aristocratic family. His grandfather Ernst was a conductor and composer. Among his teachers was Leonard Bernstein. Perhaps among the reasons for a certain discomfort was his preference for modern music, as when he dared to program the *Fourth Violin Concerto* of Alfred Schnittke for the first time with the Berlin Philharmonic in 1984.

Some musicians were amused with Horst Stein's expressive gestures and grimaces, as well as his dry humor and vulgarities. In self-irony he once remarked: 'When you look like me you have to be good,' although he looks not unattractive in some photographs. But above all he was relentlessly and agressively engaged in his work. In 1982, at the centennial of the Berlin Philharmonic, he conducted the same program with which Ludwig von Brenner had opened popular concerts of the Philharmonic on 17 October 1882 in the Bernburger Straße.

5.9   Conductors of the Twenty-first Century

When speaking of guest conductors in this century, one must make distinctions. Should we count only those in their twenties and thirties, or should also those in the fourties and older be included? It is best to spread the net widely and count already those having conducted the orchestra since the end of the 1970s. Most of them are familiar names by now and have done important work in other prestigious concert houses: Jesús López Cobos for many years with the Cincinnati Symphony Orchestra, James Levine at New York's Metropolitan Opera and the Munich Philharmonic, Claus Peter Flor with the Berlin Symphony Orchestra and the London Philharmonia Orchestra, Kent Nagano at the German Symphony Orchestra in Berlin, and many more.

Chief administrator Wolfgang Stresemann has explained how he chose younger guest conductors for whom he received suggestions every day from concert agents. They had to be outstanding talents, if not indeed geniuses, who came from good teachers, had experience in competitions, and ideally distinguished themselves in courses of conducting. It was self-evident for Stresemann that they possessed the highest technical abilities, charisma, organizational talent, ambition, intelligence, and a considerable repertoire.[24]

Members of the orchestra judge young conductors according to various criteria. For the cellist Alexander Wedow they must above all have the power of suggestion: 'The conductor gives the orchestra its identity, coaxes out of it what it has to give, awakens whatever the orchestra knows and can perform. And this spark which enlivens the orchestra,' he says, 'is also communicated to the audience during a concert.'

Others especially require of a good conductor, including the younger ones, that they present an accomplished work. They must exactly understand and interpret the content of a composition, recreate passions such as love, joy, and suffering - in short, they must have a very sensitive antenna.

For still others the most important trait of a conductor is the personal signature. The maestro should mark already established interpretations with an original insight. That requires courage, since it is not always possible to convince members of the orchestra of the quality of a different performance. Many conductors of the Philharmonic in the 21st century who have these qualities were born during the time that Karajan took over the orchestra and are thus already elders: Ulf Schirmer (born in 1958), Esa-Pekka Salonen (1958), and Christian Thielemann (1959). Simon Rattle (1955) also counts among them, perhaps as the most significant prototype of the twenty-first century.

A few words about these last conductors, except Rattle, about whom later: Ulf Schirmer received his education in Hamburg with Ligeti, Dohnányi, and Horst Stein. He was an assistant of Lorin Maazel in Vienna before he first appeared with the Berlin Philharmonic in 1993 (and again in 1995). The Finn Esa-Pekka Salonen is actually a composer, who took up the baton after no one wanted at first to perform his most provocative works. And Christian Thielemann, a native Berliner, became an assistant with Karajan, at the age of twenty-one in 1979, when he first appeared with the Philharmonic.

5.10   Without a Conductor?

This question is especially justified for an orchestra known for its fast uptake. The Berlin Philharmonic has already proven several times that it can play without a conductor, for example when giving a concert to honor one deceased. Let it be noted here, however, that some spectators have remarked that those performances did not belong to the best. Another reason for the orchestra to have played on some occasions without a qualified direction was financial. In its early years a rich sponsor would stand pro forma at the podium, thereby fulfilling a longstanding dream, but he basically only harvested what others had prepared.

In the course of the years it has also happened that some of the invited guest conductors were rather underqualified. Wolfgang Stresemann has admitted that mistakes were made in some cases, for example, by inviting singers, soloists, or very young musicians as conductors. The members fortunately knew how to compensate for such deficits at concerts.

Many musicians of the Philharmonic believe that a conductor is indispensable, above all at the inauguration of a modern work. In the score of contemporary compositions there is no unified notation, so that the artisanal intention of the composer needs to be explained (e.g., 'Here wax paper should be crumbled', or 'Imitate the sound of sawing wood'). But also to perfect some older complex works would cost more time for an orchestra without a conductor. It is not easy to reconcile the different views of about 130 players. The centrally placed conductor can better judge the whole than an individual musician, who may be separated from a colleague by as much as 25 feet. As a rule, therefore, someone to coordinate the sound is required, unlike small chamber orchestras that nearly always perform without a conductor.

6

The Berlin Philharmonic at the Festivals in Salzburg

'Salzburg during the Festivals - a jewel', declares the wife of a member of the Philharmonic when speaking of the Austrian city where the orchestra has been hosted longer and more often than in any other place during the past five decades: namely at least once and as many as three times a year, sometimes during more than a month. After the summer concerts it mostly went to Lucerne to perform during the *International Music Festival*, and a few times to festivals in Great Britain.

6.1   The History of the Festivals

It is thanks to the initiative of Max Reinhardt and some of his friends, including Richard Strauss and Hugo von Hofmannsthal, that Salzburg has become important for artists and art lovers. The summer festival was founded in 1920 as an homage to Mozart's birthplace. At first only theater and classical orchestra concerts were offered, later also opera, ballet, chamber concerts, Lieder evenings, and poetry readings. These presentations were often accompanied by congresses, exhibitions, and summer schools. Each year the mystical drama *Everyman* by Hugo von Hofmannsthal (long in a production by Max Reinhardt) stands first on the program.[1]

Only the summer events bear the title 'Salzburg Festival'. In this event the Berlin Philharmonic has almost always participated since 1957.[2] The so-called 'Salzburg Easter Festival', with an opera or two, a vocal concert, and two orchestra concerts, started ten years later at Karajan's personal initiative. Until 1989, the Berlin Philharmonic was the sole orchestra present. The impulse for the 'Whitsun Concerts Salzburg' also originated with Karajan, namely in 1973, among other reasons to allow spectators who obtained no tickets for the Easter program to attend at another time. Only in recent years the Berlin Philharmonic has no longer been part of these last concerts, although chamber music groups of the orchestra - for example, the *Berlin Baroque Soloists* - have done so under the direction of the former concert master Rainer Kussmaul.

During the three annual festivals, altogether about twice as many visitors as residents are present in Salzburg (220 000 in 1996), attracting above all youth from everywhere and filling the city with lively color.

6.2 The Festival Halls in Salzburg

Today's festival district is built on a terrain beside a mountain. Next to the buildings stands a fountain with a wall painting displaying an equestrian motif, reminiscent of the former episcopial stables of the era. There are three stages in all: one in the Great Festival House (at its dedication on 26 July 1960 it counted with its 2 179 seats among the largest and most modern in Europe); one in the Small Festival Hall; and one with nearly 1 500 seats in the *Felsenreitschule*, which is connected to the Great Festival Hall by an interior court yard. Incidentally, the Great Festival House was completed shortly before the cornerstone was laid for the Philharmonic hall in Berlin. The main impetus was provided by Karajan, who was at that time the artistic director of the Salzburg Festival.

Of the three theaters, the *Felsenreitschule* is the most striking. It is an outdoor amphitheater with a background of stone that offers an unsurpassed setting for performances. Three-story arcades penetrate into the steep slopes of the *Mönchsberg*.

Occasionally the musicians play in other concert halls of the city, for example, in the *Mozarteum* (at the University for Music and Performing Arts of Salzburg, where the Mozart archives are located), or in the centrally placed cathedral. Next to the cathedral the opening ceremony of the Salzburg Festival is held every year with an evening torch parade around the dazzling fountain.

Figure 6.1 During the Salzburg Easter Festival the inauguration of an exhibition of paintings by the orchestra member Henning Perschel in 2002, at the foyer of the Great Festival Hall.

6.3   The Supporters

Several organizations of sponsors of the festivals in Salzburg take care that the financing of music and theater is supported. The membership of the *Verein der Förderer der Osterfestspiele* guarantees the reservation of tickets for an opera, three concerts, and a special rehearsal. The rehearsal is particularly coveted because the artistic director then personally explains the concert program, reports on plans or daily operations, and tells some amusing stories. For many years the tickets for performances were in such demand that only members of these organizations of patrons could obtain them.

6.4   Berlin and its Orchestra in Salzburg

Whenever the Berlin Philharmonic took part in festivals in Scheveningen, Edinburgh, Athens, Florence, or Lucerne, it was usually not on holidays like Easter or Whitsun. That the musicians were generally in Austria on these occasions was a disappointment at home in Berlin. In the press it was repeatedly said that the orchestra should be renamed as 'Berlin Philharmonic Orchestra, Salzburg' or 'Salzburg Philharmonic Orchestra, Berlin'.

At the outset it was not easy to justify the sometimes three-week absence at Easter. Karajan argued in the 1960s that he wanted to strengthen the image of West Berlin's political predicament in international public opinion. He considered the Easter Festival, in which the Philharmonic mainly presented an opera, as a chance to create a counterweight to the Wagner Festival in Bayreuth. In fact, Karajan succeeded in convincing officials in Berlin of the Festival's importance. However, there was one difference between Bayreuth and Salzburg. In Bayreuth members of the Philharmonic had to perform during their vacation time (only a few attended Bayreuth), whereas in Salzburg playing was part of the normal duty of all orchestra members and thus, at least in part, supported financially by the Senate of Berlin.

In order to reduce the burden for Berlin, Karajan thought of something special for its annual preparations. With a record company (usually the Deutsche Grammophon) he arranged for a prior recording of the opera in Berlin. Thereby fewer rehearsals were necessary in Salzburg and a recording of the work could already be offered to the public at the premier in Salzburg.

That changed after Karajan's death. The Berlin manager Ulrich Meyer-Schoellkopf had other ideas. The opera to be presented in Salzburg would be performed by the Philharmonic in concert during the previous autumn. At the beginning of the era of Simon Rattle, the opposite occurred: the opera presented in Salzburg was performed in concert after Easter in Berlin, thus enabling the Berlin public to profit from the excursions of *its* orchestra into the repertoire of the world of opera.

6.5   A Concert Orchestra Performs Opera

Until the Easter Festival the Berlin Philharmonic scarcely had opera music on its program, in contrast to the Vienna Philharmonic, which, as the house orchestra of the Vienna State Opera, performs operas very often and complements them with concerts (in Vienna mostly as matinees or in the afternoon or on tours).

More than two dozen operas were prepared in the course of the years by the Berlin Philharmonic, among them Wagner's *Ring des Nibelungen* as well as *The Flying Dutchman*, *Tristan and Isolde*, and *Parsifal*; also Beethoven's *Fidelio*; *Frau ohne Schatten* by Richard Strauss; Verdi's *Othello*, *Falstaff*, and *Simon Boccanegra*; and several operas by Puccini, Berg,

Mussorgski, Mozart, and Britten. The Great Festival Hall in Salzburg, with its huge dimensions, is especially suitable for such presentations. It is 30 meters high behind the curtain and its stage has a width of 32 meters (compared with Vienna's opera stage that is 14 meters wide).

For some older members of the Philharmonic, Wagner's *Walküre*, with Karajan conducting, ranks as the absolute highpoint in Salzburg. After its premier the enthusiasm of the audience could not be contained. Joachim Kaiser wrote in *Die Zeit* on 24 March 1967 that this performance topped any opera in his experience and also bested the Bayreuth Festival Orchestra. In his opinion, the Berlin Philharmonic was without a doubt the best orchestra in the world. The performance of *Die Meistersinger* in 1974 was likewise widely acclaimed. Twenty-five years later, in 1999, the Berlin Philharmonic was officially honored as Germany's best orchestra for opera. Such distinctions reconcile the members of the Philharmonic with the duty of operas of 'diving' into the orchestra pit, although the managers usually see to it that the moveable orchestra platform is not sunk too far.

6.6   The Directors as Opera Conductors

Conductors naturally approach opera performances variously. Karajan functioned not only as conductor but as producer and director, occupying himself with every detail from scenery to lighting, costuming, and extras. The administrator Wolfgang Stresemann described Karajan as the 'opera director par excellence', who was initially more envolved with stage matters than with concert music.[3] And in fact Karajan was well acquainted with the repertoire of opera since the 1930s through his engagements in Ulm, Aachen, Vienna, and Milan.

Abbado had also conducted many operas early in his career, especially at Milan's Scala, New York's *Met*, the

Deutsche Oper in Berlin, London's Royal Opera House, and the Vienna State Opera. However, he left the production and stage direction to others. His concern was to realize as precisely as possible certain historical details of the composition. He suggested, for example, that for the crucial grail scene in *Parsifal* four huge bells be provided, which eerily sounded the deep 'e' note of the mystical announcement. Even Wagner had not in his time succeeded in obtaining the Chinese bells that he recommended; he had to accept enormous metal tubs that only vaguely sounded the proper tone. Since then all interpretations have had to compromise, since a church bell with a Wagnerian clang, such as could be produced in Europe, would by some calculations have to weigh 46 tons. At Abbado's performance the huge specially prepared Tibetian bells, made of light metal, came for the first time very close to the tone intended by Wagner.

Like Abbado, Simon Rattle never wanted to manage stage direction. He is rather more at home as a concert conductor. Only since the 1990s has opera appeared regularly on his programs, most of the time arranged in a very modern style. With the Berlin Philharmonic he has presented in Salzburg operas by Beethoven, Mozart, Britten, Débussy, and Wagner. The *Salzburger Nachrichten* reported in 2003 intense applause, and the *Frankfurter Allgemeine Zeitung* praised the exquisite interpretation as 'subtle, eloquent, and affecting'. He and the musicians were greeted by the audience with great enthusiasm.

6.7   The Karajans in Salzburg

In order to understand the historical roots of the Berlin Philharmonic's intense engagement in Salzburg, one needs to enter more deeply into the biography of Herbert von Karajan. He received in Salzburg his earliest education, conducted there in the *Mozarteum* his first concert, and in 1968 constructed

his private home about five miles southeast of downtown
Salzburg in the romantic village of Anif before the panorama
of the 'Untersberg', where his wife Eliette still lives.   It
therefore went without saying that the native Salzburger
would associate the orchestra from Berlin over time with this
city.

The musicians noticed that Karajan felt more relaxed
in Salzburg than elsewhere, which was evident above all at
rehearsals, where the maestro seemed more laid back than
usual and undertook his duties with more devotion. 'We are
all one big family', he sometimes remarked.

At Easter there was usually a sumptuous feast for the
members and for some guests of the Philharmonic in a giant
tent. A steer would be roasted on a spit, and beer and wine
abounded.   Japanese friends of Karajan were so impressed

Figure 6.2   Karajan and his spouse at the so-called 'Ochsenfest' in
Salzburg.

that they invited the cook along on a concert tour of Japan to assure that such an event could also be authentically celebrated in Tokyo.

The vivacious and charming Eliette was often the central figure of these feasts. Altogether the delightful lady from southern France was much loved by the orchestra. She brought out a warmer side of the otherwise strict maestro, encouraged his human qualities in relation to others, and inspired his fantasy. He had taken her as his third wife in October 1958 in the ski resort Mégève,[4] after his divorce from Anita Gütermann, the heir of the Gütermann silkwear factory. This third marriage proved to be a fountain of youth for Karajan after a child was born, since he had no offspring from the earlier two marital alliances (he had separated from his first wife, the operette singer Elmy Holgerloef, in 1941, after not quite three years of marriage). His two daughters with Eliette - Isabel (born on 25 June 1960), and Arabel (born on 2 January 1964) - are friends with many musicians of the orchestra. The Berlin Philharmonic became godfathers of Arabel, that is a representative of the orchestra was present during the ceremony of baptism.

It was not unwelcome for the orchestra that the Karajans remained an exemplary family for decades. In popular magazines their private life was frequently pictured, which automatically made the Philharmonic more known by the public. The media portrayed the maestro as a charming Austrian *bon vivant* and Eliette as an elegant and intelligent woman - both of them totally in love with their daughters. They owned a dog, and even a lama and a donkey who sometimes starred in operas at Easter. So it happened that for many years every eye in the Festival Hall was on Eliette as she took her place, almost always just before the beginning of a concert while the lights were dimming. She also shared with her husband his hobby of yoga meditation. During rehearsal intermissions at Salzburg he could sometimes been seen backstage standing on his head. She often picked him up at the festival house, exchanged a few pleasantries with others, and cared for young musicians like Anne-Sophie Mutter who, as mentioned, became over night a world star with the Berlin Philharmonic at age fourteen with a performance of Mozart's *Violin Concerto G-Major.*

6.8 Many Talents Join the Berlin Philharmonic in Salzburg

Figure 6.3 The pianist Alexis Weissenberg (right) with the former German chancellor Helmut Schmidt after a concert. Behind them, the former mayor of Berlin, Dietrich Stobbe.

Besides Anne-Sophie Mutter, who frequently performed in Salzburg between 1977 and 1986, many other instrumentalists repeatedly joined there with the orchestra. In 1986, one of them was the Franco-Bulgarian pianist Alexis Weissenberg, who had just composed his jazz musical *Nostalgie*. Karajan considered him to be one of the best pianists of the postwar era. Other 'stars' came less often. Among them was the Russian with an Islandic passport, Vladimir D. Ashkenazy, who once performed a Mozart *Piano Concerto* and Shostakovich's *Sixth Symphony* with such intense emotion that members of the orchestra were stunned by his supreme technique.

The Berlin Philharmonic of course also became acquainted with singers at Easter. Some could be engaged for several operas, such as Agnes Baltsa (six times between 1975 and 1989). In the Karajan film *Maestro, Maestro*, the mezzosoprano Christa Ludwig explains that the orchestra provided a very sensitive accompaniment for singers; it could suddenly improvise whenever anything went awry. However, Karajan's regime was rigorous: even 'star' singers were required to remain present at opera rehearsals during the whole day, often waiting for hours because a plan, on which they might have counted, did not exist. On the other hand, the maestro was very helpful for inexperienced singers: he would teach them to master their role by often taking their place during rehearsals on stage and demonstrating with suggestive gesture and voice how he wanted them to act.

Many choruses appeared with the orchestra on stage in Salzburg. There were choirs from Vienna, Stockholm, Salzburg, Bratislava, Sofia, Prague or Berlin (in 1994 the Berlin Radio Choir), as well as children's choirs from Bad Tölz, Vienna, Bozen or Zurich. Likewise, ballet troups enriched the program: from the Vienna Volksoper, the State Theater of Salzburg, and the Ballet Espagnol from Madrid. One must also mention a scenery designer who received much praise: Günther Schneider-Siemssen. A publication at the 30th anniversary of the Easter Festival proudly recalls all these collaborators, among which, after Karajan's disappearance, were several directors who set new asthetic standards: Götz Friedrich, Luca Ronconi, Herbert Wernicke, Lew Dodin, Peter Stein, and others.

After Karajan passed 75 years of age, he accepted guest conductors during his privately arranged Easter and Whitsun festivals in Salzburg.   Since 1984 at Easter Eschenbach, Tennstedt, Chailly, Giulini, Masur or Solti occasionally substituted for him at the pulpit, and at Whitsun the orchestra performed with Maazel, Ozawa, Ashkenazy or Levine.   During the later tenure of the chief conductors Abbado and Rattle, guest conductors were always welcome.

6.9   Contact with Other Orchestras

The visits of different orchestras at the summer festival in Salzburg often overlapped. Besides contacts with musicians of American orchestras, the Berlin Philharmonic had especially lively exchanges with members of the Vienna Philharmonic who had from the beginning assumed a central role in the Salzburg musical scene. One matter for discussion was the preparation by the Berliners of operas at Easter.   In 1985 it was agreed that the Vienna orchestra would repeat these performances in the summer to reduce the expense of scenery and costumes.   But at least in the initial years a slight resentment was often evident, since the Austrian orchestra perceived the performances of a competitor from the North as a kind of intrusion onto their territory.[5]

In 1987 it happened that Leonard Bernstein entered the hall with some members of the Vienna Philharmonic just as the Berliners were finishing a rehearsal.   The maestro was naturally surrounded by orchestra members from Berlin, who had many questions.   The only one who quickly departed was Herbert von Karajan, since the two conductors sometimes avoided each other like a couple of conceited prima donnas. On other occasions, however, they were seen huddled together in conversation. Then the mutual love of music was apparently stronger than a sense of competition.

A complication arose at Easter 1979. The orchestra had to interrupt its rehearsals of *Don Carlos* because the inauguration of the Berlin International Congress Center was imminent and the Berlin Philharmonic absolutely needed to be present. Originally the ICC organizers had only invited the Vienna Philharmonic, but they soon realized that Karajan would not forgive them. So the Berlin Philharmonic made a hasty trip from the river Salzach to the river Spree, where the two orchestras, from Vienna with Karl Böhm and from Berlin with Karajan, performed one after the other.

6.10   Why Musicians Enjoy Salzburg

Although members of the Berlin Philharmonic always have an extensive program of activities to manage, over the years their free time was sufficient to allow them to become well acquainted with the gorgeous landscape and the attractions of Salzburg: Mozart's birth house and residence, the late Gothic and many baroque churches and cloisters, the rose garden of the Mirabell castle, the 'Haus der Natur', and the Hohensalzburg fortress, which one can reach by a lift or on foot, whence there is a beautiful view over the city with the Salzach River and the looming mountains.

Many visitors to the festivals combine their stay with an extended vacation, despite the frequent and often persistent rain showers. They bring cosmopolitanism and enthusiasm to this otherwise bucolic region - not to speak of an elegance more obvious in Salzburg than elsewhere. A sort of highbrow folklore in Salzburg is offered by costumed music groups with their so-called *Stubenmusik*, frequently composed by plain citizens of the Salzburg area, for example the *Mindl-Walzer*, a piece written by a native farmer. Even in small churches one might hear a Mozart mass, otherwise unusual in religious communities of this size.

Naturally the folks of Salzburg are proud to have housed so many celebrities over time: Carl Zuckmayer, Stefan Zweig, Curd Jürgens, and Helmut Kohl, to name only a few. Karajan and Abbado as well as other orchestra members were delighted to ski in the mountains at Easter. They all enjoyed the specialties of local cuisine, particularly the Salzburg dumplings made with egg white and the *Mozartkugeln* whose recipe famously has its origin in Salzburg.

Like Karajan, several members of the Philharmonic had a dwelling in Salzburg-Anif. From there it is not far to Hellbrunn with its castle and beautiful park, which contains a zoo much appreciated by the musicians with small children. For a long time it was possible to admire in that zoo a pair of lions named 'Herbert' and 'Eliette' after the Karajans. On the meadows around Anif may stand storks, or hawks can be seen in the trees, and at night the wolves howl. Local pubs also contribute to the friendly atmosphere. However, the Karajan neighbors sometimes expected too much from him, for instance a new pipe organ once the old one expired. The maestro did donate a new electronic organ with stereo system in 1969, but the church's flock longed to have a classical pipe organ as before, which was obtained in 1980 through public donations. This was one instance in which local residents felt estranged from their famous countryman.

6.11 Karajan's Honors in Salzburg

Many of Karajan's birthdays on April 5 coincided with the Easter Festival. There was sometimes a party for him, but the maestro generally found such celebrations to be unpleasant. To stress the normality of such days, he would rigorously carry out the customary rehearsals mornings and afternoons in spite of his numerous other obligations.

Of his birthdays, two - his 60th in 1968 and his 80th in 1988 - were especially noteworthy. On the former, the orchestra awarded him the Golden Ring of the 'Comradship' of the Berlin Philharmonic (now called the 'Association') and he was named an honorary citizen of Salzburg. As for the latter birthday, the orchestra presented *Tosca* in the Great Festival Hall, after which the maestro with his wife and his daughter Arabel sat on the stage while they were showered with speeches. Furthermore he received copies of Peter Gelb's film *Karajan in Salzburg* and Peter Csobádi's large anthology of memoirs entitled *Karajan or the Controlled Ecstasy*. The Deutsche Grammophon also released a collection of twenty-five CDs with a hundred works that Karajan had recorded with the orchestra. Each CD was decorated with paintings created through the years by Eliette in her studio, thereby melding the fruits of her passion with those of her husband.

Figure 6.4   CD envelopes with paintings by Eliette von Karajan.

6.12   Karajan's Death in Salzburg-Anif

The circumstances of Karajan's death on 16 July 1989, about three months after his 81st birthday, and of his burial thereafter, have been related by several residents of Anif. Because of various infirmities in previous years, the conductor was often carefully attended by his wife without his being bedridden for long periods. Preparations for the Summer Festival of 1989, in which he was to participate, were well underway in July.

On Saturday the 15th the maestro conducted a stage rehearsal of Verdi's *Masked Ball*, and on the next morning he received at home the president of Sony, Norio Ohga (who once had studied vocal music in Berlin), as well as the director of the Sony-Corporation in America, Michael Schulhof. Eliette had just returned from her daily bike ride and was in another room as Ohga called her. Karajan's death was due to heart failure. A Catholic priest, who happened to be with relatives at a neighboring house, hurried over, but he could do no more than offer last rites.

Now the question was how to conduct the funeral in peace. Photographers and journalists would surely not leave the tiny cemetery of Anif intact. Karajan had years before purchased a burial plot right next to the chapel. A crowd of press reporters would certainly not be acceptable. Someone had the idea to hold the actual burial on the next day while giving official notice that it would be on some later day at another place.

Hence the gravediggers began their work on the next day. But when they struck a stone base under the earth's surface, where a monument had stood, the burial could not begin until after the base was removed by a tractor and forklift at 9 p.m. About a dozen persons were present that evening, including the next of kin, plus their servant Francesco, the village priest of Anif and his colleague, and also the current proprietor of the restaurant 'Goldener Hirsch', Count von Walderdorff. For a long time thereafter speculations made the rounds about the reason for the rather hasty burial service. The deception had succeeded.

The maestro's grave by the cemetery church was initially decorated with a simple wooden cross. That is what members of the Philharmonic saw after arriving as planned for the summer concerts in Salzburg. For the performances of 27 and 29 August 1989 they played Verdi's *Requiem* under the direction of Riccardo Muti (who also owns a home in Anif). Further memorial concerts followed, the first one in Berlin on 10 September 1989 in the Great Hall of the Philharmonic, where the veteran manager Wolfgang Stresemann gave a moving speech. On 6 May 1990 the 'Society of Friends of the Berlin Philharmonic' staged an evening of chamber music with the 'Nomos Quartet' and the invited solo clarinettist Sabine Meyer. And finally, memorial concerts were held at the Easter Festivals in Salzburg in 1991, 1993, 1998, 1999, and 2008. In 1999, on the 10th anniversary of Karajan's death, *Mozart's Requiem* was conducted in the cathedral by Claudio Abbado, his first successor. And in 2008 Beethoven's *Violin Concerto* was played by Anne-Sophie Mutter under the direction of Seiji Ozawa on the occasion of Karajan's 100th birthday.

During the summer of 1990, the musicians from Berlin saw in Salzburg that Eliette had arranged for an iron cross from southern France and a single white stone with Herbert von Karajan's name and dates. Since 2001 a bust of Karajan stands on the street beside the cemetery. In a certain sense, the large Sony factory in Anif-Niederalm also recalls his memory as one of the first to recognize with Sony's founder the importance of CDs for music. Many residents of the Salzburg vicinity have work there - or in a second factory in Thalgau - where several of the old Karajan recordings are still reproduced.

Some streets, squares, and halls have been named after Herbert von Karajan: for instance, in Salzburg the square beside the Great Festival Hall; in Berlin the street in front of the Philharmonic hall as well as the reception hall of the Austrian Embassy; in Ulm, where he was active for a long while, the square in front of the Municipal Theater; likewise in Linz, a main street; in Anif, the street behind Karajan's house; and in Tokyo, a square in the Suntory business complex (see p. 79) - to name only a few.

Vienna honors the maestro also in this fashion with the square situated beside the State Opera. In that city his memory was equally preserved for ten years by the *Herbert von Karajan Center*, an organization acting separately from Berlin's *Herbert von Karajan Foundation*. The former emerged in 1995 from the *Télémondial Foundation*, founded by Karajan in 1989, and served to further the various interests of the conductor. Funds from this organization were used, besides building a Karajan archive, to support research in music and medicine, to encourage young instrumentalists, and to carry out a rich cultural program. Since 2005 the center has moved to Salzburg, where it has been rebaptized as the *Eliette and Herbert von Karajan Institute.*[6]

Whenever the Berlin Philharmonic visits Salzburg, one or another of the players can be seen standing in the cemetery, lost in thought. During tours of the festival grounds, Karajan's name is always mentioned. And in the many Salzburg souvenir shops CDs, books, pamphlets, and printings with Karajan's picture and name are still in demand.

Even without all of that, the man who was for many years celebrated as the greatest conductor of classical music would not disappear from memory. At the already noted memorial concert in Berlin in September 1989, the Philharmonic played among other pieces the second movement of Schubert's *Unfinished Symphony*. The empty pulpit seemed desolate as never before.

6.13   The Festivals since 1989

After the death of the maestro, many questions remained for the Easter Festival and the Whitsun Concerts, which, unlike the Summer Festival, were personal initiatives of Karajan and depended on his financing them. Should they continue and, if so, would the public flock to them even without Karajan? Should they in the future, as before, feature the Berlin Philharmonic, or should the Vienna Philharmonic, which was on better terms with Karajan before his death, take over? It was moreover still to be decided, in case the Berliners continued, who would direct the concerts before the introduction of a new candidate as chief conductor.

Figure 6.5 One of the Salzburg Easter concerts was a charitable event, entitled 'Neighbor in Need', for wartorn Yugoslavia: moderator Peter Ustinov (l.) stands beside Georg Solti and Claudio Abbado.

To avoid as many difficulties as possible, the business manager of the Easter Festival, Beate Burchhard, strongly advocated that the Easter Festival be extended with the Berlin Philharmonic. Her proposal was accepted: Salzburg without the Berlin Philharmonic, everyone agreed, would be unthinkable. However, for Easter 1990, the orchestra had already arranged for an invitation to Israel and was therefore unavailable for the first year. Starting in 1991 the musicians appeared at first under Bernard Haitink (at that time musical director of London's Covent Garden Opera), and under Daniel Barenboim, who then frequently conducted the orchestra. In the 1992/93 season, Georg Solti signed on as interim director of the Easter Festival and the Whitsun Concerts.[7] The latter were continued without the Berlin Philharmonic.

In 1993 decisions to continue in Salzburg Karajan's former links to the Berlin Philharmonic were sealed by a public ceremony in which the musician Christhard Gössling presented an enormous bouquet of flowers to Eliette von Karajan, now honorary head of the company organizing the Easter Festival. In 1994 Claudio Abbado took over direction of the Easter Festival, and since 2003 the director is Simon Rattle.

6.14   Salzburg Awards for the Orchestra

Two awards document how significant is the participation of the Berlin Philharmonic at the festivals in Salzburg. At the 50th anniversary of the Summer Festival in 1970, every member of the orchestra received the Max Reinhardt medal. On one side is a portrait of Reinhardt, the great director who founded the Festival, on the other the Latin motto: 'Sacra camenae domus concitis carmine patet' ('The muse of this sacred house is open to whoever has art in his heart').

At the hundredth anniversary of the orchestra in 1982, the governor of the Salzburg district, Wilfried Haslauer, presented the second award, a 60-pound bronze plaque honoring 25 years of participation to the festivals in Salzburg. It has been cemented into the wall of the south foyer of the Philharmonic building in Berlin. At the dedication ceremony Haslauer read aloud a text, found during excavations necessary for the erection of a Mozart monument in the old city of Salzburg. It once adorned a Roman temple: 'Here happiness thrives; may evil never enter'.

'There is for a German-speaking instrumentalist no higher goal than to become a member of the Berlin Philharmonic. It is rather similar to the Vienna Burgtheater for German-speaking actors, the Milan Scala for Italian singers, and Hollywood for the film world.' (Friedrich Herzfeld)

7

Present and Future with Sir Simon Rattle

The twenty-first century began for the musicians of the Philharmonic already in 1999 with the choice of 44-year-old Englishman Sir Simon Rattle as the successor to Claudio Abbado. Since then several projects have been realized that changed the organizational and artistic structure and point to the future. As mentioned before, one of the changes in 2002 was that, on records or during concerts, the name of the orchestra is now one, namely *Berliner Philharmoniker*.

7.1 The Berlin Philharmonic Foundation

The decision concerning the name came along with the transition from a publically subsidized institution to a foundation largely supported by private business money.[1] Since then, the orchestra has undertaken in all organizational questions more responsibility than before. This was particularly pronounced from October 2003 to July 2006 because the initial manager, Franz Xaver Ohnesorg, unexpectedly and prematurely left Berlin, and because a new

Figure 7.1 Organizational transformation into a foundation in 2002. Here Simon Rattle (r.) after the signing of a contract with the representative of the Deutsche Bank, Josef Ackermann.

chief administrator could not quickly be found. Not until August 2006 did Pamela Rosenberg take over the role of chief administrator.

7.2   Simon Rattle as Chief Conductor

With Sir Simon Rattle, who is a very direct person with great energy and an appealing charisma, the atmosphere changed. He expresses his opinions lucidly and effectively. The musicians do not depend on suggestions and hints. Raised like the Beatles in Liverpool from 1955 into the 1970s, and musically educated on an instrument rare for a conductor of classical music, the drums (but also with instruction in piano, violin, and bass strings), he meets the members of the Philharmonic more as an equal. This is why they just call him Simon. His talent to put everyone at ease is remarquable.[2]

That is especially true of rehearsals. His often humorous manner of explaining what he wants expresses youthful charm. Christian Stadelmann, leader of the second violins, puts it as follows: 'Simon Rattle attempts to avoid a rigid face-to-face situation between orchestra and conductor. Music must be exciting, it must be fun. The fantastic magic of Karajan still exists today, but in a totally different fashion.' While polishing certain passages, the maestro spontaneously leaves his pulpit to join individual instrumental groups in order to offer better advice - something unthinkable for Karajan and seldom with Abbado. He shows great patience with everyone, a trait seen by members of the orchestra as a guarantee for a healthy atmosphere. It is a collegial, respectful, and relaxed collaboration. In 2008, a considerable extension of his initial contract (which started in 2002) beyond the planned ten years was approved by a great majority.

7.3 Website: *Zukunft@BPhil*

As for the orchestra's website, which gives detailed information about programs, music, employment openings, tours, reviews in the press, etc., it was earlier operated according to the latest fashion than those of other orchestras. Concertgoers can choose their tickets online with all manner of suggestions and discussions, and past programs since 1945 are kept in a data bank, for the time being only for internal use. There one may quickly find, for example, a record of the many conductors and soloists who have appeared with the Berlin Philharmonic, including the dates of their performances and the programs.

A special novelty of the website since the Rattle era is the concept *Zukunft@BPhil*. It represents the engagement of the orchestra for youth and marginal groups. Since 2002, individual members of the Philharmonic, the chief conductor, and several teachers have devoted attention to an educational project for potential listeners and aspiring musicians. They lead mainly youngsters between ten and eighteen to classical music (sometimes older from underprivileged social circumstances) by inspiring them to take up playing, composing, conducting, dancing, or film-making with musical themes. The entire orchestra then appears with them. The atmosphere of this work is strikingly documented in the film *Rhythm is it!*. To some degree this is the continuation of Karajan's effort in education. But whereas he emphasized university graduates as music students who received further training of the Berlin Philharmonic through his *Orchestra Academy*, it is now essentially a matter for younger pupils of lower and middle class.

Thus, through *Zukunft@BPhil*, the Philharmonic has become, by comparison to earlier, a more vital and active factor in the city's public life, above all because the project contains a social component. Many underprivileged youth as well as adults are approached, such as those from poor families,[3] also the handicapped living in hostels, even convicts who heretofore have had little opportunity to experience live classical music and were scarcely motivated to do so. Music is performed in unaccustomed forms - followed by discussions, films, or lectures - and in unusual places, for instance, in former factories like the 'arena Berlin' situated in a working-class section of the city. The object is to integrate persons with no great musical understanding or artistic talent in order to awaken their creativity.

Tessen von Heydebreck, longtime chief administrative officer of the Deutsche Bank (which is a main financial sponsor of this project), has commented: 'The halo of the orchestra can also intimidate.' To avoid that is part of the program's objective, which is to counter the gradual erosion of cultural learning. As Simon Rattle confirms: 'Music is not a luxury but a basic nourishment for every human.' Decades before, during the Second World War, the orchestra had already experienced that music can have a healing effect under unfortunate circumstances. Even then concerts were sold out, since classical music made life more bearable for many in the audience.

7.4   Increased Media Attention

Another innovation since the outset of the Rattle era has been the more prominent role of the orchestra in the landscape of film, television, press, and internet. The chief conductor and the Philharmonic's public relations and media officials have increasingly undertaken special initiatives. When Sir Simon assumed his position in Berlin in the 2002/2003 season, placards with his portrait appeared everywhere in the city. He understands how to showcase the orchestra during interviews with humor, optimism, and faint self-irony. The Berlin Philharmonic's own magazine, more luxurious than before,

Figure 7.2 Each year the final concert of the season is held at Berlin's *Waldbühne*.

is distributed for free, along with programs, brochures, and announcements. Recordings are no longer made as a rule without an audience but in the concert hall. Performances are sent over television and over internet (see the orchestra's webpage under *Digital Concert Hall* [4]). Film productions are organized. A first documentary film with music of the Berlin Philharmonic arrived at cinemas in January 2004, the Dolby presentation for giant screen entitled *Deep Blue*, with breathtaking photography of the oceans and a musical score directed by the composer George Fenton. It was acclaimed as an audiovisual delight. Another combination of music and cinema was Oliver Herrmann's silent film *Le Sacre du Printemps* with music by Igor Stravinsky played by the Berlin Philharmonic. Thereafter Simon Rattle conducted the Philharmonic's recording of a musical score for the film *Das Parfum*, based on a novel by Patrick Süskind. When it was shown at its premier, an impressive atmosphere of sensuality fascinated everybody in the audience.

7.5   Novelties in Style and Program

When taking over the direction of the orchestra, it was important for Sir Simon to broaden the Philharmonic's range of sound. As he has emphasized in interviews, he attempts to attain a bright, fresh, transparent tone in which the baritone instruments clearly emerge. For many works he has been able to communicate this vision to the entire orchestra, apparently with ease and with relatively few rehearsals.

As for the construction of the orchestra's programs, the maestro is concerned to continue the trend of the 1990s. Already at that time, elsewhere as in Berlin, he considered it as his assignment to free baroque music from the domination of ancient music specialists and also to make certain pre-classical works available for the orchestra. At the same time, his goal was to add to the program many modern pieces that had previously been heard seldom or not at all. Right after his selection of chief conductor, that is, three years before his official inauguration, he formulated his intention to pursue these trends.

In the meanwhile, a number of these objectives have been realized. In the category of old music, chamber works have been integrated with symphony concerts, thereby introducing pieces by baroque masters like Purcell, Rameau, Bach, Händel, and Jean-Féry Rebel, often performed with ancient instruments, for example, the viola da gamba. Rattle's greatest accomplishment, observed the *Münchner Merkur* on 5 April 2004 regarding an opera presentation of the Berlin Philharmonic in Salzburg, was that the orchestra played 'as if it had always employed historical performance techniques'. Some have pointed out that Claudio Abbado had likewise moved in this direction. Others believe that it has to do with Rattle's experience with the *Orchestra of the Age of Enlightenment*, for which he is a regular guest conductor.

In the category of contemporary music, many unknown works have been introduced within a few years, more than ever before,[5] awakening the public's understanding of tonality, cacophony, and cluster by serving up 'distasteful morsals' - following the old proverb that pleasure comes with familiarity. The orchestra has commissioned several new works such as the jazz-like composition of Heiner Goebbels,[6] who was for a time composer-in-residence (see p. 96). Hence, light and serious, classical and popular music are mixed - no wonder with a talent versatile like Rattle who knows to communicate in a dynamic way. As he said to a journalist of the Berlin *Tagesspiegel* on 29 December 2003: 'Classical music may again be for enjoyment.' And he added: 'What is serious? What is fun? For me it is all the same.' The Englishman is convincing that modern classical music still has the power to move our media-saturated world, which is almost a commonplace in a city like Berlin with its international public and highly sensitive feeling for everything futuristic.

Sometimes composers alter their score while working in rehearsals with the orchestra in Berlin, especially whenever they reach the limits of instrumental possibilities. In such cases the act of creation is partially shared by the Philharmonic. Proposals to include more works by women, as well as Asian or Latin American composers, have been realized, e.g., in the 2003/2004 season compositions by the female Finnish composer Kaija Saariaho and the Chinese Tan Dun, or in 2008 by a series of concerts called *Alla turca*.

Withal, it is of course true, as always, that the great mentors of past centuries have not been neglected. In the order of frequency, the most performed composers up to the year 2000 have been Beethoven, Mozart, Brahms, Tchaikovsky, Richard Strauss, Haydn, Stravinsky, Dvořák, Bruckner, Schumann, Schubert, and Mendelssohn-Bartholdy.[7] With scarce modification, the trend of this distribution remains constant. No doubt, the task of a great classical orchestra is to demonstrate the continuing modernity of these composers and therewith to prevent a general historical deficit. Some more seldomly played classics by Hindemith or Furtwängler have since 2000 gained wider public acceptance through outstanding performances.

Introductory presentations before actual concerts prepare the public for performances in the concert hall. These often take the form of lecture-concerts in which the conductor or other people explain musical particularities with examples. Such illustrations loosen up and sharpen the ear of the audience, creating an intimacy between orchestra and public.

7.6   Chamber Music Ensembles

The rich repertoire of the Philharmonic is augmented by its nearly thirty chamber musical organizations, whose names are

available on the orchestra's website. Most members are quite
active in such small groups, some indeed in several. 'In the
Philharmonic there are many generals', says one musician.
'In chamber groups they are better able to express their
own musical interpretation; here there is less anonymity.'
Some presentations are benefit concerts. Besides appearing
in concert halls, chamber musicians also play on ceremonial
occasions, for example, at the burial services for politicians
or actors. The surroundings at such events are not always
ideal. As the actress Hildegard Knef was carried to her grave
in Berlin, the weather was cold and instruments had to be
protected from the gathering rain.

During a few years since 1997 several chamber music
groups have participated in so-called 'marathons' at the
Philharmonic, at which chamber works of a specific composer

Figure 7.3 The former German chancellor Helmut Kohl (left) - and
at his side the parliamentarian Klaus Bühler - after a chamber concert
of the orchestra's ensemble *Divertimento Berlin.* In the background
the musicians Siegfried Schäfrich (l.) and Stefan Jezierski, to the right
Wolfgang Güttler.

were especially honored in workshops with simultaneous lectures and performances in the chamber music hall, in the lobby, and in the music rooms of the Philharmonic. Opulent buffets were served during pauses. Now chamber music groups play during the regular lunch concerts on Tuesdays, where people have to pay no entrance fee.

Some chamber music ensembles are named according to their featured instruments, such as the *Philharmonic String Octet Berlin* or the *Drummers of the Berlin Philharmonic*. Others have less obvious names. The instruments of the *Venus Ensemble Berlin*, for example, are violins, violas, cellos, sometimes a piano - whereby the word *Venus* indicates that only females are members of this group. They organized themselves in 2002 'in order to assault the bastion of chamber music still dominated by men'.[8]

Personnel changes arise often in such intimate groups, since it only becomes clear after a while who suits whom. Fluctuations likewise occur because a musician moves to another city, a person retires or dies, and also through offers of collaboration with other musicians. Several chamber music groups have meanwhile been dissolved, for instance the fourteen-man *Haydn Ensemble*, the six-man *Philharmonic Chamber Soloists*, the *Bastiaan-Quartet*, the *Brandis-Quartet*, and the *Westphal-Quartet* (these last three named after the violinists Johannes Bastiaan, Thomas Brandis, and Hanns-Joachim Westphal).[9]

The Twelve Cellists is one of the most successful chamber music groups. Its founder Rudolf Weinsheimer[10] organized in June 1992 an immense cello festival in Potsdam, attended by 341 cellists from the entire world who performed on a warm summer evening in front of Potsdam's impressive New Palace. The conductor was Gernot Schulz, a percussionist of the Berlin Philharmonic, joined by retired and active members of the orchestra. In 2001 this group received in Los Angeles the Grammy Award, the so-called Oscar of Music, for its CD with South American compositions, as well as the German recording prize *Echo Klassik.*

Most of the chamber music ensembles listed on the website exclusively comprise members of the Berlin Philharmonic. But in some instances independent musicians or those from other orchestras belong to a group, such as the twelve-man *Berlin Baroque Soloists* founded in 1995, or those belonging to the *Berlin Philharmonic Jazz Group* that exists since 1999.[11] A few members of the Philharmonic play in groups unlisted on the internet under the name of the orchestra. Such is the case of the solo flutist Andreas Blau who founded the *14 Berlin Flutists*, a chamber music association since 1996 that is composed mostly of musicians who are not members of the Philharmonic.

Figure 7.4 The chamber music group *The Twelve Cellists.*

7.7 Musical Guests in the House of the Berlin Philharmonic

Since the Berlin Philharmonic does not give concerts daily in the German capital, it sometimes rents its building to other artists. In recent times the number of guest appearances by orchestras, choirs, or soloists in afternoon or evening performances has reached two hundred annually.[12]

There is a special relationship with some of the guests, for example, the *Young German Philharmonic*, an organization that has grown out of the *Federal Student Orchestra*. Members of the Philharmonic especially take young people under their wing when these are in Berlin, that is, they give them advice in daily rehearsals, setting programs, planning tours, and they also lead practice sessions of individual instrument groups. But in the great concert hall also more worldwide known orchestras have been heard such as the *Vienna Philharmonic* - the great rival of the Berlin Philharmonic. In April 2005 the two orchestras gave a joint concert.[13]

The Philharmonic building is likewise frequently used by numerous other Berlin classical orchestras. Especially ensembles that have available no concert hall, or a very small one, often attempt to book one of the Philharmonic facilities when the house orchestra is on tour. Among them is the *German Symphony Orchestra Berlin* with its 112 musicians, which was founded in 1946 as the *West Berlin Radio Orchestra RIAS* (longtime with Kent Nagano as chief conductor), and also the *Radio Symphony Orchestra Berlin*, founded in 1923, which was for many years in the former East zone of the city (it has about 70 musicians, for many decades under the chief conductor Marek Janowski). The *Berlin Symphonists* with 65 musicians, long under the direction of Lior Shambadal, is also on occasion a guest at the Philharmonic, as are the three opera orchestras of the city that can be heard there whenever they present symphony concerts. Besides many other smaller groups, the impressive *Konzerthausorchester Berlin* with its 108 musicians has played in the Philharmonic hall (its usual house is Schinkel's concert hall on the Gendarmenmarkt).[14] One may add the *Symphonic Orchestra of Berlin* with its 71 musicians.

For laymen these many similar orchestra names are confusing. Yet one thing is clear: visiting concerts in the house of the Berlin Philharmonic profit from the internationally recognized host orchestra's reputation.

7.8 An Open Ambiance

What more could one wish? Perhaps improvements on the Philharmonic's urban surroundings and its internal architecture. On the outside traces of the Berlin Wall atmosphere remain, leaving a deserted appearance throughout the daytime despite a central location. The entrance and the lobby, because of being classified as a monument, are stuck with the flair of the 1960s. It seems that future changes have already come under consideration in the direction of loosing up the rather deserted area of what is called the district of the *Kulturforum*, which comprises several museums and the National Library.

First, relatively easy steps to create a more lively house have been undertaken. Daily tourist visits (not merely on Saturdays as before) are offered at 1 p.m., as well as explanations by tour guides during concert intermissions. During day time, school classes, students, and teachers may use the facilities for educational purposes by joining certain rehearsals or training exercises. The annual gathering of Berlin school orchestras brings in more life each autumn. Here Sir Simon knows how to conquer the heart of the young people with a few jesting instructions like 'the violins sound too English, not sexy enough' or 'the drums are too soft, please a little more Schwarzenegger'. Since 2003 there has been a 'Day of the Open Philharmonic', during which tours to every corner are conducted (including to some rooms otherwise only used by musicians), turning the house into an excited scene for culture lovers or just curiosity seekers. Amusements include open rehearsals, concerts, and exhibitions as well as the expanded Philharmonic Shop in the lobby and a modernized restaurant area.

For evenings other changes have been made. An inviting lighting illuminates the flag-bedecked entrance to the building. Here and there small groups like singers with accompaniment, child musicians, or jugglers appear and beg a pittance for their presentation - something unthinkable until a few years ago. Even youngsters on roller skates are tolerated on the large marble surface in front of the building. At the entrance near the ticket counters there are occasional mini-concerts by members of the Philharmonic (for instance violins accompanied by a pianist), so that those who do not obtain a ticket can imagine what they are missing. Even some conductors do not consider it beneath their dignity to appear there to discuss with the public, as did Pierre Boulez on 17 March 2004. Three days before a concert, anyone short of cash can purchase tickets cheaply for the benches behind the orchestra, provided the performance does not include a vocal chorus. Thus Rattle's motto that classical music should be for everyone is gradually becoming a reality.

Also contributing to this end is the annual concluding concert at the great open-air theater of Berlin's *Waldbühne*. More than 22 000 gather there in June at the end of each musical season to experience a sort of happening in a natural setting. People sit on benches or blankets, consume red wine with cheese or other delicacies, and listen to the music, whatever the weather - often at the end of the concert by candle light. For many of them the Waldbühne concerts are the highpoint of their musical adventure for an entire year. 'We come because the same notes sound different here,' said one participant, 'and to share a collective experience in which everyone seems to be silently in harmony. Also to be very close to the sounds of heaven.'

A regular to the concerts of the Berlin Philharmonic, Giuseppe Vita, who is since 2001 in the directorate of the Schering firm and since 2002 on the council of the Philharmonic Foundation, has stated his enthusiasm for the orchestra in the following words: When he and his family arrived in Berlin and spoke little German, the Philharmonic became his second home. 'Because we all understand,' said the Italian, 'the language of music.'[15]

8

Notes

Preface

[1] The Japanese version of this book, translated by Hideaki Mogami and edited in Tokyo in 2007 by alphabeta-publishing company, is in its 3rd edition. During the preparation of the original German version, which has been revised since 2005, there were only one scolarly book and one picture book available in the stores: The three volumes of Peter Muck's *Einhundert Jahre Berliner Philharmonisches Orchester. Darstellung in Dokumenten*, Tutzing: Hans Schneider Verlag 1982; and the picture album by Reinhard Friedrich (with 12 pages of text by Joachim Matzner) *Die Berliner Philharmonie. Philharmoniker, Dirigenten, Solisten*, Berlin: G + H Verlag 1999. Meanwhile, mostly due to the 125th anniversary of the Berlin Philharmonic, prepared since 2005 and celebrated in 2007, and because of Karajan's 100th anniversary in 2008, several other publications have appeared: in 2005 twelve CDs with comments by journalists of *Die Welt* and *Welt am Sonntag* entitled *Berliner Philharmoniker - Im Takt der Zeit*; in 2006 five DVDs entitled *Berliner Philharmoniker. 125 Years - A Jubilee Celebration.* (with 45 pages of comment by Tobias Möller); in 2007 two audio cassettes: *Die Orchesterrepublik - Ein Streifzug durch die Geschichte der Berliner Philharmoniker*; plus two volumes of the book *Variationen mit Orchester. 125 Jahre Berliner Philharmoniker*, Berlin: Henschel Verlag; and also Herbert Haffner's book *Die Berliner Philharmoniker. Eine Biografie*, Mainz: Schott Verlag 2007. As for the many publications on Karajan's 100th birthday, see footnotes in chapters 2 and 6.

Chapter 1

[1] Letter from Richard von Weizsäcker, former president of the German Federal Republic, to the author, 27 January 2005.

[2] See Edgar Wisniewski, *Die Berliner Philharmonie und ihr Kammermusiksaal. Der Konzertsaal als Zentralraum*, Berlin: Gebrüder Mann Verlag 1993; the small volume of Johannes Althoff, *Die Philharmonie*, Berlin: Berlin Edition 2002; and *Rückblick, Augenblick, Ausblick. 40 Jahre Berliner Philharmonie*, Berlin: Berliner Philharmonie GmbH 2003.

[3] The concert house at the Gendarmenmarkt, all but the front wall, was destroyed in the Second World War and was not reconstructed until 1984.

[4] On the seating arrangement of orchestras, see Friedrich Herzfeld, *Magie des Taktstocks. Die Welt der großen Dirigenten, Konzerte und Orchester*, Berlin: Ullstein 1953, pp. 110-111; and Ermanno Briner, *Reclams Musikinstrumentenführer*, Stuttgart 1998, 3d ed., pp. 589-608 (the sketches on the seating order presented in this book are taken from Briner).

[5] Ideally the note 'a' has 440 vibrations per second. But in many cases the orchestra agrees to an 'a' above that (443 or even 445 vibrations).

[6] On 16 March 1882 the musicians separated from Benjamin Bilse and founded an organization with a three-man directorate and a democratic format. The first artistic director was Ludwig von Brenner. The group became independent on 1 May 1882 and assumed the name of *Philharmonic Orchestra* on 17 October 1882. See the publications of the Benjamin Bilse Society; see also Friedrich Herzfeld, *Die Berliner Philharmoniker*, Berlin: Rembrandt Verlag 1960; and Werner Oehlmann, *Das Berliner Philharmonische Orchester*, Kassel: Bärenreiter Verlag 1974.

[7] Concerning the non-accord of Karajan and the orchestra on certain votes, see Werner Thärichen, *Paukenschläge. Furtwängler oder Karajan*, Zurich, Berlin: M & T Verlag 1987.

[8] The Siemens family is known for its generous support of classical music. Already in the year 1883 it offered a grant to aid the orchestra in its

beginning. The Siemens Villa in Berlin, a princely building with a huge park, was acquired by Werner Ferdinand von Siemens in 1925. He had a concert hall constructed. During the 1940s, Ernst von Siemens - head of the Deutsche Grammophon - spent many hours in conference with Karajan. Now the Siemens Villa houses the German Music Archive.

[9] Since Abbado's nomination, journalists have proposed the comparison with a papal election. To the question of what his election as chief conductor of the Berlin Philharmonic meant to him, Simon Rattle responded: 'It is somewhat as though I had been elected Pope.' (Dieter David Scholz, *Mythos Maestro*, Berlin: Parthas 2002, p. 260).

[10] In 2002-2003 the Berlin Philharmonic had a staff of 80 administrators (see the 312-page memorandum of the orchestra entitled *Berliner Philharmonie*). Before the construction of the Philharmonic building there were less than 10 administrators.

[11] The *Association of the Berlin Philharmonic* was founded in 1890 in order to establish a pension fund. After 1938 the state took over insurance for the musicians (see Gerassimos Avgerinos, *Das Berliner Philharmonische Orchester als eigenständige Organisation. 70 Jahre Schicksal einer GmbH. 1882-1852*, Berlin 1971). Currently the *Association of the Berlin Philharmonic* is above all responsible for affairs of human interest concerning the musicians.

[12] For a long time the royalties for music recorded with Karajan were important for each musician because the basic salary was low in comparison with salaries of other musicians of that quality. Still today the royalties from these recordings are remarkable.

[13] On the interwar years and the early time of National Socialism of the Berlin Philharmonic, see Misha Aster, *'Das Reichsorchester'. Die Berliner Philharmoniker und der Nationalsozialismus*, Munich: Siedler Verlag 2007 (turned into a documentary movie by E. Sanchez Lansch).

[14] Let us mention here the *Intendanten* (chief administrators) of the orchestra. From autumn 1933 to december 1934: Rudolf von Schmidtseck; from January 1935 to summer 1939: Hans von Benda and Karl Stegmann; from autumn 1939 to summer 1945: Gerhart von Westerman; from autumn 1945 to summer 1951: no *Intendant*; from autumn 1951 to summer 1952: Eduard Lucas; from autumn 1952 to

summer 1959: Gerhart von Westerman; from autumn 1959 to summer 1978: Wolfgang Stresemann; from autumn 1978 to summer 1984: Peter Girth; from autumn 1984 to summer 1986: again Wolfgang Stresemann; from autumn 1986 to summer 1989: Hans Georg Schäfer; from autumn 1989 to summer 1990: Ulrich Eckhardt; from autumn 1990 to summer 1996: Ulrich Meyer-Schoellkopf; from autumn 1996 to summer 2001: Elmar Weingarten; from autumn 2001 to december 2002: Franz Xaver Ohnesorg; from 2003 to July 2006: no *Intendant*; from August 2006 to 2010: Pamela Rosenberg.

[15] It was never known whether the clause 'for life' was contained in Karajan's contract. In public, the Senator for Science and Culture, Joachim Tiburtius, always mentioned it only vaguely ('more or less for life'). Karajan's successors were unable to negotiate such terms: Claudio Abbado at first received a seven-year contract, later extended for five years; and Simon Rattle began with a contract for ten years (until 2012), which was extended in 2008 for at least ten years.

[16] On the complicated circumstances of Furtwängler's position as artistic director in the period from 1934-52 see Klaus Lang, *„Lieber Herr Celibidache ... " Wilhelm Furtwängler und sein Statthalter - ein philharmonischer Konflikt in der Berliner Nachkriegszeit*, Zurich and St. Gallen: M & T Verlag 1988. After the war, pending an explanation of his role in the Hitler regime, Furtwängler was at first prohibited from conducting. Not until May 1947 was that again possible. During the interim, Celibidache had Furtwängler's position. See Erich Hartmann, *Die Berliner Philharmoniker in der Stunde Null. Erinnerungen an die Zeit des Untergangs der alten Philharmonie*, Berlin: Feja Verlag 1996.

Chapter 2

[1] Quoted from *Das Berliner Philharmonische Orchester* (with pictures by Tim Rautert and 13 essays by different authors), Stuttgart: Deutsche Verlagsanstalt 1987, p. 154.

[2] See the picture album *Herbert von Karajan*, with a preface by Klaus Geitel, Braunschweig: Westermann 1984; see also the picture books by Pierre-Henri Verlhac, *Herbert von Karajan. Bilder eines Lebens*,

with essays by Anne-Sophie Mutter and Jürgen Otten, Berlin: Henschel Verlag 2007 (also published in French); and the picture album by Erich Lessing, *Herbert von Karajan*, with an introduction by Rainer Bischof, Vienna, Cologne, Weimar: Böhlau Verlag 2008.

[3] Karajan's first appearance in the hall of the Berlin Philharmonic was reviewed by Heinrich Strobel in the *Berliner Tageblatt*, 10 April 1938.

[4] Wolfgang Stresemann, ... *und abends in die Philharmonie. Erinnerungen an große Dirigenten*, Frankfurt and Berlin: Ullstein 1994, p. 150.

[5] See Richard Osborne, *Herbert von Karajan. Leben und Musik*, Vienna: Paul Zsolnay Verlag 2002, p. 650 (published as a pocketbook in Munich by dtv in 2008). He documents in detail the earnings from records with EMI in 1964. In the first quarter of that year Karajan stood in fourth place with this firm with 10 903 pounds sterling – behind the Beatles (with 46 982 pounds), Cliff Richard, and The Dave Clark Five. Maria Callas was in fifth, Dietrich Fischer-Dieskau in seventh, and Otto Klemperer in eighth place.

[6] Ibid., p. 753.

[7] See W. Stresemann, *„Ein seltsamer Mann ... ”: Erinnerungen an Herbert von Karajan*, Berlin: Ullstein Verlag 1990, 2nd edition 1999, and pocketbook 2008.

[8] The exact name of the institute is *Herbert von Karajan Akademie für Weiterbildung in künstlerischer Psychotherapie und Musiktherapie*. It is part of the Herbert von Karajan Foundation.

Chapter 3

[1] Quoted from Christian Försch, *Claudio Abbado. Die Magie des Zusammenklangs*, Berlin: Henschel Verlag 2001, p. 177.

[2] See Ulrich Eckhardt (ed.), *Claudio Abbado. Dirigent*, Berlin: Nicolai 2003, pp. 18 - 27.

[3] The self-awareness of the orchestra is described by Dieter Blum, Emanuel Eckhardt, *Das Orchester. Herbert von Karajan und die Berliner Philharmoniker*, Dortmund: Harenberg Kommunikation 1988. The pictures by Dieter Blum later led to a volume published on

the occasion of the 125th anniversary of the orchestra: *Berliner Philharmoniker*, ed. by Wolfgang Behnken and Jürgen Dormann, Wachter: Ed. Braus, May 2007, 216 p., German and English.

[4] Frithjof Hager, *Claudio Abbado. Die anderen in der Stille hören*, Frankfurt: Suhrkamp 2000. There are also two video tapes by Paul Smaczny (Stuttgart: Euroarts International) with Abbado's portrait bearing the titles *Die Stille nach der Musik* (*The Silence after the Music*), 1996 and *Die Stille hören* (*Listen to the Silence*), 2003.

[5] In a film of the television channel ARTE, entitled *Maestro, Maestro! Herbert von Karajan*, Seiji Ozawa relates that he would never have dared to address his honored master as *Herbert*, not even when, after many years, Karajan proposed the familiar form 'Du'. The solution was to address him simply as *Maestro* rather than, as before, *Herr von Karajan*. See the book to the film by Claire Alby and Alfred Caron, *Karajan, l'homme qui ne rêvait jamais*, Paris: Editions mille et une nuits 1999.

[6] *Musica sopra Berlino. Conversazione con Lidia Bramani* (Milan: Bompiani 1997; translated into German: *Musik über Berlin*, Frankfurt: Axel Dielmann Verlag 2001) is one of a dozen publications by Abbado.

[7] The themes are described by Habakuk Traber, in *Claudio Abbado. Dirigent*, Berlin 2003, pp. 137-158; also by Annemarie Vogt, *Warum nicht Beethoven? Repertoire und Programmgestaltung des Berliner Philharmonischen Orchesters 1945-2000*, Berlin: Mensch und Buch Verlag 2002, pp. 157-174.

[8] See Helge Grünewald in *Das Berliner Philharmonische Orchester mit Claudio Abbado*, (with pictures by Cordula Groth) Berlin: Nicolaische Verlagsbuchhandlung 1994, pp. 94-117; see also Cesare Colombo (pictures)/ Enrico Regazzoni, Ermanno Olmi (text), *Accordi. Claudio Abbado ed I Berliner Philharmoniker*, German and Italian, Milan: F. Motta 1997.

[9] Note an article in the *Frankfurter Allgemeine Zeitung*, 20 Dec. 1997.

Chapter 4

[1] Already under Furtwängler the number of visiting concerts exceeded those performed in Berlin. During Abbado's twelve-year contract as

artistic director he conducted 296 visiting concerts but only 286 in Berlin. See U. Eckhardt, *Claudio Abbado...*, op. cit., p. 10.

[2] In the early years with Furtwängler the musicians often traveled fourth class in trains. They went to Moscow over night without sleeping car and to Scandinavia on small vessels. Hotels were also not always first class and at times included youth hostels. Nowadays, with long trips to various cities, the costs soar to several hundred thousand dollars. Comfort is guaranteed - as for colleagues from Vienna or New York.

[3] Most *Europe Concerts* are meanwhile available on DVD. The first ten of these are documented by Cordula Groth (pictures) and Wolfgang Thormeyer (text): *Musik für Europa. 10 Jahre Europa-Konzerte zum 1. Mai*, Berlin: be.bra Verlag 2000.

[4] The Berlin Philharmonic also played outdoor concerts three years after Epidauros (September 1968) in the Bacchus Temple of Baalbek in Lebanon, and later in the Hollywood Bowl in Los Angeles. Regarding presentations at Berlin's Waldbühne, see p. 140.

[5] Some experts call this concert hall 'the most adorable of all older music halls' (M. Forsyth, *Buildings for Music*, Cambridge: MIT Press 1985).

[6] Hellmut Stern, *Saitensprünge. Erinnerungen eines Kosmopoliten wider Willen*, Berlin: Aufbau Verlag 2002, 3rd edition.

[7] The 'Abbadiani Club' was founded in 1995 with the intention to create an Abbado Archive in Milan. The archivist is Rosemary Ripperger. The Club has about 200 members.

[8] Quoted by Harald Eggebrecht, *Große Geiger*, Munich and Zurich: Piper 2001, p. 31.

[9] Hans von Bülow, who has been called the 'first significant fully professional conductor in the world' (Herbert Haffner, *Orchester der Welt*, Berlin: Parthas 1997, p. 75), initially came to Berlin in 1882 with the Court orchestra of Meiningen. In 1884 he debuted with the Berlin Philharmonic.

[10] The solo drummer Rainer Seegers is a butterfly collector, the violinist Gustav Zimmermann - who contributed many pictures to this book - a collector of insects. In Japan, Zimmermann had the chance to find an unknown species, which was called after him *stenus zimmermanni puthz*. When Karajan heard about it, he congratulated him for the

discovery in a note of recognition written into his first biography
(Ernst Haeussermann, *Herbert von Karajan*, Wien, München, Zurich,
Innsbruck: Fritz Molden 1978) which had appeared during that time.

[11] Karajan's membership in the Nazi Party was debated in political
hearings in 1946. He explained that, despite his membership, he
was in disfavor with its leadership. In 1942, after he had married
Anita Gütermann who had one Jewish grandparent, he had suffered
disadvantages: His appearances in Bayreuth, Salzburg, and Vienna,
as well as in the neutral countries Switzerland and Sweden had been
cancelled. On orders from the SS and the Party he had been rejected
as the successor of Karl Böhm at the Dresden Opera, after having been
forced to resign as director of the Berlin State Opera in 1942. Moreover,
in contrast to his colleagues, he had not been invited to official receptions
and had received none of the usual tax breaks, cars, houses etc. In 1944
there had been a 50 percent reduction of his salary as conductor of the
so-called 'Philharmonic Concerts' at the Opera House in Berlin (see R.
Osborne, pp. 925-936). Also in 1944 the ministery of propaganda had
refused to pay a honorarium to Karajan for a concert planned in Paris
and to deliver a visa for his wife. See the telegrams of May 4 and 24,
1944 in the archives of the Ministry of Foreign Affairs in Berlin, quoted
by Allan Mitchell, *Nazi Paris. The History of an Occupation 1940-1944*,
New York, Oxford: Berghahn Books 2008, p. 202.

[12] Wolfgang Stresemann describes the initiative of 1965 to give a concert
in Israel in *Zeiten und Klänge*, Frankfurt, Berlin 1994, pp. 321-322; as
for the initiative in 1967, see Hellmut Stern, *Saitensprünge*, pp. 276-
278. Both relate that Karajan was not unwilling to tour Israel with
the Berlin Philharmonic. Eberhard Diepgen, mayor of Berlin from 1984
to 1989 (and again 1991 to 2001), suggested a trip by the orchestra to
Israel in 1984. But Stresemann considered this timing to be unfavorable
because of the Sabine Meyer scandal.

Chapter 5

[1] W. Stresemann, „*Ein seltsamer Mann* ... ", Frankfurt and Berlin 1999
(2nd ed.), p. 16.

[2] In 1982 Peter Muck (op. cit.) records 948 conductors who have appeared with the orchestra since its founding. During the 2002/2003 season the orchestra performed with 22 guest conductors.

[3] It was at that time assumed that Karajan avoided contact with Bernstein, perhaps out of jealousy over Bernstein's abilities as a composer, perhaps from anger with his remarks over Karajan's role during the Hitler regime.

[4] Christa Ludwig remarks in her autobiography that Bernstein - like Karajan - was one of those rare conductors whose interpretation could be recognized on radio even by the untutored listener (Christa Ludwig, ... *und ich wäre so gern Primadonna gewesen*, Berlin: Henschel 1994, pp. 74-75).

[5] See Karlheinz Roschitz in *Dirigenten*, Vienna: Österreichischer Bundesverlag 1986, p. 30.

[6] Quoted by Ernst Krause in *Große deutsche Dirigenten*, Berlin: Severin und Siedler 1981, p. 76 (the father of Richard Strauss was solo hornist at the court theater in Munich). Böhm's motto in his later years was: 'I should not be sweating but rather the public.'

[7] The program included Mozart's *Symphony No. 25* and his *Concert for Clarinet and Orchestra A-Major* as well as Schubert's *Symphony No. 5*. Peter Muck's book has to be corrected in this detail.

[8] On candidates discussed as possible successors to Karajan, see Norman Lebrecht, *Der Mythos vom Maestro*, Zurich and St. Gallen: M & T Verlag 1992; and Dieter David Scholz, *Mythos Maestro*, Berlin: Parthas Verlag 2002; see also Peter Cossé's essay in *Das Berliner Philharmonische Orchester*, 1987, op. cit., p. 14.

[9] On Bernard Haitink's relation to the orchestra, see Helge Grünewald, in: *Bernard Haitink. Liber Amicorum* (ed. Paul Korenhof), Amsterdam: Anthos 1999, pp. 73-82.

[10] Karl Schumann in *Das Berliner Philharmonische Orchester*, 1987, op. cit., p. 53. Mehta's debut in Berlin occurred in 1961.

[11] See Helga Schalkhäuser, *Riccardo Muti. Begegnungen und Gespräche*, Munich: Langenmüller 1994.

[12] See the critique of Maazel by W. Stresemann, *Zeiten und Klänge*, op. cit., p. 176.

[13] Hans-Klaus Jungheinrich, *Die großen Dirigenten*, Düsseldorf: Econ Taschenbuch Verlag 1986, p. 148.

[14] Among Ozawa's presentations of Japanese composers in Europe was *November Steps Number I* (1970) by Toru Takemitsu, the world premier of Ishii Maki's *Polarities for Soloists and Orchestra* (1973), and Anjo Keis's *Who-ei* (April 1989).

[15] Karl Schumann in *Das Berliner Philharmonische Orchester*, 1987, op. cit., p. 46.

[16] Among the most prominent guest composers of the orchestra - who conducted their own works - were Johannes Brahms (1884 to 1897), Peter Tchaikovsky (first on 8 February 1888), Richard Strauss (in 1894 for one year as artistic director and later for 50 years as guest conductor), Gustav Mahler (for example in 1895 and 1907), Stravinsky, Prokofieff, Shostakovich, Bartók, and Paul Hindemith (for example on 18 February 1934).

[17] W. Stresemann, „*Ein seltsamer Mann ... *", op. cit., p. 189/190.

[18] In the series *Music of the Twentieth Century* Henze directed the premier of his *Barcarola für großes Orchester* in the Philharmonic. He was 'composer in residence' during the 1991-1992 season (see also Annemarie Vogt, op. cit., p. 96).

[19] Annemarie Vogt (op. cit.) has evaluated that, among the composers whose 'works have remained in the program for years' and who are even increasing in popularity were Mahler (2,14 %), Hindemith (1.67 %), Bartók (1.88 %), and Prokofieff (1.45 %).

[20] See Daniel Barenboim, *Die Musik - mein Leben*, Berlin: Ullstein Verlag 2002.

[21] Up to 2005 only seven females conducted the Berlin Philharmonic: Mary Wurm in 1887, Eva Brunelli in 1923, Ethel Leginska in 1924, Lise Maria Mayer in 1929, Antonia Brico in 1930, Marta Linz in 1930, and the Swiss Sylvia Caduff (born 1937) in 1978. In March 2008, Emmanuelle Haïm and Susanna Mälkki were guest conductors of the orchestra. On female conductors see Elke Mascha Blankenburg, *Dirigentinnen im 20. Jahrhundert. Porträts von Nadia Boulanger bis Simone Young*, Hamburg: Europäische Verlagsanstalt 2003.

[22] Norman Lebrecht, *Der Mythos vom Maestro*, op. cit., p. 109.

[23] Karl Schumann in *Das Berliner Philharmonische Orchester*, 1987, op. cit., p. 44.

[24] W. Stresemann in *Das Berliner Philharmonische Orchester*, 1987, op. cit., p. 192. On the qualities of a good conductor see also Harold Schonberg, *Die Großen Dirigenten*, Bern, Munich, Vienna: Scherz Verlag 1973, pp. 18 and 21.

Chapter 6

[1] Isabel von Karajan, the older daughter of Herbert von Karajan, is a professional actress. She sometimes played a leading role in the opening theater play of the Salzburg Festival.

[2] See *Die Salzburger Festspiele*, Salzburg: Residenz Verlag 1991; and Hans Landesmann and Gerard Rohde (eds.), *Das Neue, Ungesagte. Salzburger Festspiele*, Vienna: Paul Zsolnay Verlag 2002. The Berlin Philharmonic was not present during the summer festivals of 1958-59, 1961, 1963, 1965, 1967, 1969, 1971, 1984, 1996, 1998, and 2002.

[3] W. Stresemann, „*Ein seltsamer Mann* ... ", p. 66. At the Easter Festival in Salzburg, Karajan found 'the realization of his opera dreams', writes Klaus Lang, *Herbert von Karajan. Der philharmonische Alleinherrscher*, Zurich and St. Gallen: M & T Verlag 1992, p. 83.

[4] Eliette Mouret met Karajan aboard a yacht at Saint-Tropez in the 1950s. At the time she was not yet twenty years old and worked as a model for Dior and others. See her autobiography *Karajan. Mein Leben an seiner Seite*, Berlin: Ullstein 2008 - in French *A ses côtés*, Paris: Editions l'Archipel-France Musique 2008. See also Pierre-Jean Rémy, *Karajan, la biographie*, Paris: Editions Odile Jacob 2008; Peter Uehling, *Karajan. Eine Biographie*, Reinbek: Rowohlt Verlag 2006 - also in French - Paris: Editions Hermann Musique 2008; and Roswin Finkenzeller, *Das Phänomen Karajan*, Frankfurt: Societätsverlag 2008.

[5] When the Berlin Philharmonic was first engaged at the Salzburg Festival in 1957, it was a 'Salzburg shock' among the Vienna Philharmonic, writes the musician Otto Strasser, *Und dafür wird man noch bezahlt ... Mein Leben mit den Wiener Philharmonikern*, Vienna and Berlin: Paul Neff Verlag 1974, pp. 292, 321.

[6] The archive houses information about 3 300 opera and concert performances as well as all the recordings of Karajan. A music shop offers a wide variety of literature and old discs.

[7] After Karajan's death, Solti took over the direction of Verdi's *Masked Ball*, planned for the Salzburg Festival in the summer of 1989. From 1993 to 1995 Solti shared direction of the Easter Festival with Claudio Abbado. Since 1998 the Whitsun Concerts are directed by the organizers of the summer festival.

Chapter 7

[1] On the financing of the 'Stiftung Berliner Philharmoniker' see Manuel Brug, quoted by Nicholas Kenyon, *Abenteuer der Musik. Simon Rattle*, Berlin: Henschel Verlag, 2nd ed., 2007 (revised by Frederik Hanssen).

[2] Following are a few details of Rattle's life. He debuted at the Berlin Philharmonic on 14 November 1987 with Mahler's *Sixth Symphony* while he was still chief conductor of the City of Birmingham Symphony Orchestra and frequently guest conductor of the Orchestra of the Age of Enlightenment and of the Birmingham Contemporary Music Group. He regularly came to the Berlin Philharmonic after 1989 (up to five times a year). His contract as chief conductor there was signed on 19 September 2001. As for his private life, he is reluctant to talk about it. His first wife was the American soprano singer Elise Ross, with whom he has the two sons Sacha (born 1984) and Eliot (born 1989). His second wife (from 1996 to 2001) was also an American, Candace Allen, whose uncle, Luther Henderson, was an arranger for Duke Ellington. His last partner is the young mezzo soprano singer Magdalena Kožená with whom he has two children (born 2005 and 2008). He lives with them in his house in Berlin-Nikolassee.

[3] In Venezuela the conductor José Antonio Hebreu started a similar initiative some years ago when he addressed children from the 'favellas', whom he gave bread and clothes after they agreed to play or sing music. He thus formed a huge orchestra and a choir. In the 19th century, a similar initiative was started by the conductor Benjamin Bilse, some of whose musicians formed the nucleus of the Berlin Philharmonic in 1882.

154   8 Notes

Bilse founded a 'Musik-Lehrinstitut' for children from poor families
where they got a free music education.

[4] The *Digital Concert Hall* is the first initiative of its kind in the
world of classical music. People around the world are enabled via
internet to experience the concerts of the Berlin Philharmonic as they
are happening. For the direct access to one concert the fee does not
exceed 10 euros.

[5] Several modern composers have been invited to the Philharmonic:
Thomas Adès, Sidney Corbett, Matthias Pintscher, Mark-Anthony
Turnage, Brett Dean, Johannes Maria Staud, Magnus Lindberg, Detlev
Glanert, and others.

[6] Rattle likes jazzmusic. Both of his parents played piano jazz. He
himself was often engaged as drummer in a jazz orchestra and produced
an album, entitled *Classic Ellington*, with the City of Birmingham
Symphony Orchestra

[7] For the period from 1945 to 2000 the percentage of the most played
composers was calculated by Annemarie Vogt (op. cit.): Beethoven
(9.96 % of all concerts), Mozart (9.07 %), Brahms (5.68 %), Tchaikovsky
(3.32 %), R. Strauss (3.28 %), Haydn (3.17 %), Stravinsky (2.87 %),
Dvořák (2.79 %), Bruckner (2.53 %), Schumann (2.53 %), Schubert
(2.32 %), and Mendelssohn (2.16 %) (the percentage of works played
by Bach was only 1.62 %).

[8] On the *Venus Ensemble*, which varies in seize (4 to 15 female
musicians), see *BERLINER PHILHARMONIKER - das magazin*,
March/April 2004, pp. 38-39. For them music of female composers
is welcome but not necessary (for example, in 2003 they played the
Second String Quartett by the Russian composer Sofia Gubaidulina).
The atmosphere in this group is relaxed because 'the sometimes rather
strenuous situation between females and males, which distracts from
essential tasks, does not exist'.

[9] The violinist H.J. Westphal emphasizes that, due to the large number
of compositions written for string quartetts, the foundation of string
ensembles is obvious. There are fewer works written only for flutes or
drums. Chamber orchestras for those instruments are thus bound to
play scores specially arranged for them or to wait for new compositions

to appear.

[10] Rudolf Weinsheimer, one of the two leading officers of the Berlin Philharmonic from 1978 to 1984, founded the *Twelve Cellists* in 1974. More than forty works were dedicated to that group. See the humorous website of this ensemble, also the volume by W. Stresemann, *Die Zwölf*, Zurich: Atlantis Musikbuchverlag 1982, and the article in *BERLINER PHILHARMONIKER - das magazin*, May/June 2004, pp. 22-25.

[11] On the *Berlin Philharmonic Jazz Group*, see Jan Verheyen in *BERLINER PHILHARMONIKER - das magazin*, Dec. 2002/Jan. 2003, pp. 26-27.

[12] For orchestras having appeared in the hall of the Berlin Philharmonic, see for the years 2002 to 2005 the annual *Preview of all Presentations* published by the Berlin Philharmonic; and, for the time thereafter, the annual program preview.

[13] The Vienna Philharmonic was founded in 1842. It first appeared before a Berlin audience in 1918.

[14] The *Konzerthausorchester Berlin* has a similar attendance as the Berlin Philharmonic, namely, about 98 % of capacity. In 1990 the audience of the Berlin Philharmonic was altogether nearly 200 000. Both orchestras have between 17 000 and 20 000 regular subscribers, and both give nearly hundred public concerts per year in Berlin, plus twenty to thirty on tour.

[15] Quoted from *BERLINER PHILHARMONIKER - das magazin*, May/June 2004, p. 55.

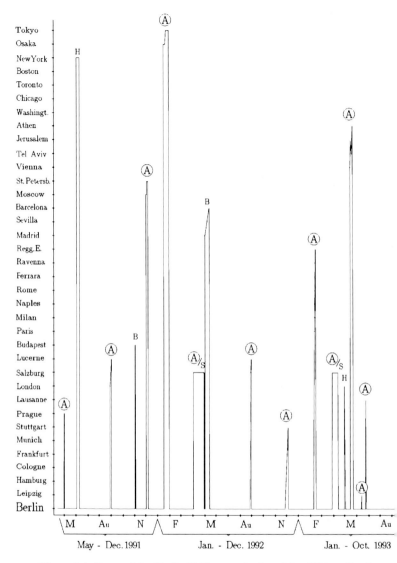

Figure 8.1 Tours of the Berlin Philharmonic from May 1991 to October 1993, during which the orchestra went on 18 trips to 36 cities. Claudio Abbado (**A**) conducted 14 times, Daniel Barenboim (**B**) and Bernard Haitink (**H**) did so twice each. On two occasions Georg Solti (**S**) shared the program with Abbado at Salzburg, in April 1992 and 1993.

Index